Engineering

Engineering

Other books in the Careers for the Twenty-First Century series:

Careers
for the
Twenty-First
Century

Engineering

by Mark and Sherri Devaney

**LUCENT
BOOKS**

THOMSON
™
GALE

San Diego • Detroit • New York • San Francisco • Cleveland
New Haven, Conn. • Waterville, Maine • London • Munich

SENECA MEDIA CENTER

On cover: An engineer carries out her responsibilities at a petrochemical plant.

© 2003 by Lucent Books. Lucent Books is an imprint of The Gale Group, Inc.,
a division of Thomson Learning, Inc.

Lucent Books® and Thomson Learning™ are trademarks used herein under license.

For more information, contact
Lucent Books
27500 Drake Rd.
Farmington Hills, MI 48331-3535
Or you can visit our Internet site at http://www.gale.com

LIBRARY OF CONGRESS CATALOGING-IN-PUBLICATION DATA

Devaney, Mark
   Engineering / by Mark Devaney and Sherri Devaney
      p. cm. — (Careers for the 21st century)
Summary: Describes the job outlook and required training, education, and
qualifications for engineering career opportunities in business, telecommunications,
and many other fields.
Includes bibliographical references and index.
   ISBN 1-56006-897-3 (hardback : alk. paper)
   1. Engineering—Vocational guidance—Juvenile literature. [1. Engineering—
Vocational Guidance. 2. Vocational guidance.] I. Devaney, Sherri. II. Title. III. Careers for
the 21st century (San Diego, Calif.)   620.0023
  TA157 .D42 2003   DEVANEY
  620'.0023—dc21   CC
                             2002008116

Printed in the United States of America

Contents

Foreword

Young people in the twenty-first century are faced with a dizzying array of possibilities for careers as they become adults. However, the advances of technology and a world economy in which events in one nation increasingly affect events in other nations have made the job market extremely competitive. Young people entering the job market today must possess a combination of technological knowledge and an understanding of the cultural and socioeconomic factors that affect the working world. Don Tapscott, internationally known author and consultant on the effects of technology in business, government, and society, supports this idea, saying, "Yes, this country needs more technology graduates, as they fuel the digital economy. But . . . we have an equally strong need for those with a broader [humanities] background who can work in tandem with technical specialists, helping create and manage the [workplace] environment." To succeed in this job market young people today must enter it with a certain amount of specialized knowledge, preparation, and practical experience. In addition, they must possess the drive to update their job skills continually to match rapidly occurring technological, economic, and social changes.

Young people entering the twenty-first-century job market must carefully research and plan the education and training they will need to work in their chosen career. High school graduates can no longer go straight into a job where they can hope to advance to positions of higher pay, better working conditions, and increased responsibility without first entering a training program, trade school, or college. For example, aircraft mechanics must attend schools that offer Federal Aviation Administration–accredited programs. These programs offer a broad-based curriculum that requires students to demonstrate an understanding of the basic principles of flight, aircraft function, and electronics. Students must also master computer technology used for diagnosing problems and show that they can apply what they learn toward routine maintenance and any number of needed repairs. With further education, an aircraft mechanic can gain increasingly specialized licenses that place him or her in the job market for positions of higher pay and greater responsibility.

In addition to technology skills, young people must understand how to communicate and work effectively with colleagues or clients from diverse backgrounds. James Billington, librarian of Congress, ascertains that "we do not have a global village, but rather a globe on which there are a whole lot of new villages . . . each trying to get its own place in the world, and anybody who's going to deal with this world is going to have to relate better to more of it." For example, flight attendants are increasingly expected to know one or more foreign languages in order to better serve the needs of international passengers. Electrical engineers collaborating with a sister company in Russia on a project must be aware of cultural differences that could affect communication between the project members and, ultimately, the success of the project.

The Lucent Books *Careers for the Twenty-First Century* series discusses how these ideas come into play in such competitive career fields as aeronautics, biotechnology, computer technology, engineering, education, law enforcement, and medicine. Each title in the series discusses from five to seven different careers available in the respective field. The series provides a comprehensive view of what it is like to work in a particular job and what it takes to succeed in it. Each chapter encompasses a career's most recent trends in education and training, job responsibilities, the work environment and conditions, special challenges, earnings, and opportunities for advancement. Primary and secondary source quotes enliven the text. Sidebars expand on issues related to each career, including topics such as gender issues in the workplace, personal stories that demonstrate exceptional on-the-job experiences, and the latest technology and its potential for use in a particular career. Every volume includes an Organizations to Contact list as well as annotated bibliographies. Books in this series provide readers with pertinent information for deciding on a career, and a launching point for further research.

Careers in Engineering

The world would be impossible to imagine without engineers. In fact, the world today is largely a product of the imagination of engineers. And the world of tomorrow will be shaped greatly by the minds and hands of future engineers.

Engineering is a career without limits, yet it is also a career that people, especially young adults, know little about. Many current engineers confess that they did not know that they wanted to be engineers until they attended college. If they had known sooner about engineering, they would have better prepared themselves for the job market, and they would have suffered less anxiety about the question: "What do you want to be when you grow up?"

There are well over one hundred engineering specialties, but in general there are five major disciplines: electrical, mechanical, civil, chemical, and industrial. Each of these differs in many ways, yet all share aspects that are basic to all engineering disciplines.

What Is Engineering?

According to Raymond B. Landis, author of *Studying Engineering: A Road Map to a Rewarding Career,* a book about engineering for college students, "Engineering is essentially the application of mathematics and science to develop useful products or processes."[1] The engineering profession, however, is defined not so much by what it is as by what it has produced. And to discover what engineers have produced, all one needs to do is open his or her eyes.

Simple items like paper clips and massive structures like the Sears Tower in Chicago were made by engineers. Lifesaving devices like flame-retardant baby pajamas and fetal heart monitors would not be here without the brilliance and dedication of engineers. Clothing and food, ranging from genetically grown cotton to instant oatmeal, are not cultivated or cooked as much as they are engineered by engineers. Real weapons used in war and virtual weapons found in arcades are made possible because of engineers. What was once thought of as extraordinary has become ordinary thanks to engineers who make robots that can do what humans cannot do and spacecraft that launch humans to the moon and across the solar system.

More than Math and Science

The two core subjects all engineers must master are math and science. To most engineers neither math nor science is daunting. Typically, engineers enjoy math and science and are happy to have a career that allows them to apply what they know about these subjects on a daily basis.

It is safe to say that all engineers start out with either an aptitude for or an interest in math and science, which could include algebra, geometry, calculus, chemistry, biology, and physics. Yet unlike

Skyscrapers like Chicago's Sears Tower are among the most impressive testaments to the ingenuity of engineers.

mathematicians and scientists that spend the majority of their careers exploring theoretical aspects of these subjects, engineers seek to apply theory to real world situations.

Although math and science are key subjects for all engineers, they are by no means the only important subjects. What a lot of young engineers do not realize until they begin working professionally is that communications courses like English and public speaking are incredibly important.

It is a falsehood that engineers sit behind a desk all day in front of a computer working on math problems. The truth is that engineers write reports more than they add and subtract numbers. Many engineers have to make important presentations in public, which requires good communication skills and an ability not only to explain complicated engineering matters, but to persuade people to accept something that they may not like. Engineers deal in facts, and sometimes the facts can be disturbing. While explaining a complicated technical scenario or presenting a controversial idea, engineers count on communication skills that are not taught in math and science classes.

Problem-Solving Teams

Engineers also should not be confused with inventors or scientists, who sometimes work alone in workshops and laboratories. Although engineering is primarily a technical profession requiring an individual to think about challenging subjects and complicated problems, an engineer seldom works in solitude.

Behind every product and service, behind every invention and innovation, behind every technology and tool, stands a team of engineers. Often that team is comprised of engineers from different disciplines, each bringing an equally important perspective to a problem that can be solved only through input from all team members. Like virtually every other profession—athletics, law, medicine, and politics—engineering requires teamwork, so the ability to cooperate is critical for all engineers.

Engineers working in teams solve confounding problems. They know how to ask the right questions and arrive at the right solutions to overcome the obstacles that leave most people befuddled. For some engineers technological know-how comes naturally. Others have to work at it. Regardless, all engineers must complete a rigorous course of study at engineering-accredited universities or colleges in order to become an engineer.

However, the learning does not stop once a degree is achieved. Engineers are constantly educating themselves to keep on top of the latest technologies. In a way, graduation for engineers is not so much the finish line as it is the starting point. The best engineers often say that learning never stops, so engineering is a career for someone with an insatiable appetite for knowledge.

Well-Rounded Career

For their ability to solve seemingly impossible problems, engineers are much admired and much sought after by companies that want an edge against competitors. Annually, companies send recruiters to college campuses seeking qualified prospective engineers. Those who have good grades and demonstrate a particular specialty tend to be valuable and usually have no trouble finding employment with impressive starting salaries.

Yet, although engineers can make an immediate impact in a company and are paid well, they cannot afford to remain complacent. Engineers who do not evolve and grow with a company may find other engineers making more money than them down the road. One way to avoid this potential problem is to keep going to school to earn additional degrees or degrees in different engineering disciplines. No engineer is locked in for life to one discipline. For example, engineer Steve Donati graduated with a degree in mechanical engineering, but worked for ten years as a civil engineer before becoming an environmental engineer, which required getting a Professional Engineer credential. Another engineer started as a ceramic engineer, then obtained a degree in biomedical engineering, and finally a Ph.D. in mechanical engineering.

Additional degrees can also be secured in nonengineering fields. Some engineers go on to law school and others get a Master of Business Administration (M.B.A.) degree, which helps them attain a business leadership position in their company and ultimately receive a higher salary.

Despite the earnings potential of engineering, for some reason the profession has long suffered unfairly from the stigma of being for "brains" only. Engineers often mention how they had to overcome being labeled a "geek" or a "nerd" as they persevered to become successful professionals. However, that stigma is slowly fading. Some engineers have even become celebrities.

Of course, fortune more so than fame finds most engineers. But making money is only part of the equation. Contrary to popular opinion, engineering is not a one-dimensional job for technically minded people. It is much more than that. It is a career that leads to challenging work that changes the world, provides personal fulfillment and lifelong friendships, and pays a rewarding salary that grants financial security.

Chapter 1

Electrical Engineering: Robots, Radio Waves, and Solar Panels

More so than any other field of engineering, electrical engineering touches everything because electricity is the most critical element of most technologies. The fundamental knowledge of electrical systems possessed by electrical engineers serves as the foundation of many important networks in the world today: communications networks, including telephone, cable, the Internet, and wireless; the power networks used to generate electricity; and the much smaller networks found in machinery and miniature devices.

Whether it is a futuristic robot, a modern automobile with a complex computer system, or the latest handheld video game, electrical engineers come up with the circuitry that allows these things to operate. Electrical engineers have changed and continue to change the world in many ways. They are intelligent and creative thinkers dedicated to improving life and business through the power of electricity and networking systems.

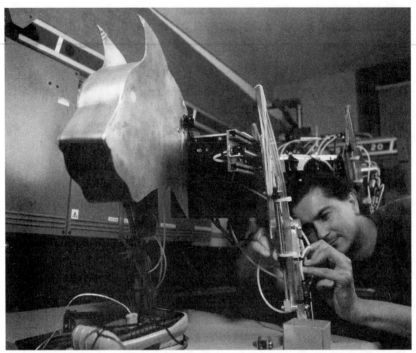

An electrical engineer fine-tunes the circuitry of a cat robot. Electrical engineers design the components that control the operating systems of many such high-tech devices.

The Power of Electricity

During the past century people all over the world have relied more and more on electricity. In the future, electrical energy will continue to be the key energy form for the majority of all activities at work and at home. For example, the so-called "digital economy" that relies on the Internet to communicate and conduct business is electrically powered.

Electrical engineers are at the forefront of any project that develops the tools and equipment designed to improve our lives. Today's electrical engineers use the latest technologies to come up with new time- and money-saving applications. Time and money, as well as safety, are key considerations in any electrical engineering project, because electrical engineering, like all fields of engineering, has a strong connection to business.

Tools for Business

Electrical engineers develop technological tools that help companies run operations more efficiently and safely. For example, robots are tools that can help a company reduce the amount of time it takes to complete difficult tasks and keep employees out of harm's way. Two such robots named Rover and Scavenger are used to inspect and clean nuclear reactors, preventing humans from being exposed to dangerous radiation.

Although Rover may have a dog's name and something like a dog's leash, it is made from a high-density polyethylene plastic and equipped with special gaskets that will not leak after being placed in nuclear reactor water. Rover was originally designed for deep-sea diving expeditions, but was modified by a team of engineers led by Harry Roman, an electrical engineer and senior technology consultant at a leading power utility company.

Rover's job is to visually inspect the fuel rods and chambers of a nuclear reactor submerged in radioactive water. Roman describes Rover as "a pair of flying eyeballs shaped like a torpedo that went around checking the condition of the walls inside the nuclear reactor through video and by taking pictures. We were very nervous at first because this type of solution had never been done before using robotics, but Rover performed flawlessly."[2]

Rover does not work alone. Scavenger, another robot modified by Roman's team, also goes underwater. Scavenger vacuums the floors of the fuel pool so that when new fuel is moved into the reactor it will not bring debris into the reactor pit. It is critical to remove debris before new fuel fills the chamber, otherwise the debris could loosen and float into the reactor pit, causing serious damage to the system. Rover and Scavenger perform jobs more quickly than humans, which saves utility companies money and time; but most important, by going into dangerous radioactive water like the fuel pool of a nuclear reactor, these robots help keep employees safe.

Money-Saving Machines

Engineers are not simply inventors; they are hired to solve specific problems with innovative products or processes that will ultimately make or save money for the companies that employ them. According to Harry Roman, "You just don't build something because you can. You build something because ultimately someone will buy it."[3]

Rover and Scavenger, two of the six robots developed by Roman's team, are good examples of how electrical engineering plays a key role in improving business through robotics. Roman's robots, which cost a total of $1.8 million to build, have saved his company alone well over $10 million to date.

Roman also was approached by representatives from a robotics development team and asked to apply his electrical engineering expertise to build a robot to help solve the problem of inspecting and cleaning the insides of large oil tanks without having to drain them first, a costly and difficult process. Roman's team met the challenge with a robot named OTIS (Oil Tank Inspection System), which is now used all over the world in the huge oil tanks found along highways as well as on oil tankers at sea. Roman explains: "Based upon what we learned from Rover and Scavenger, our team went on to develop a new device that can visually inspect the floors and walls of oil tanks using ultrasonic scanners that can detect any thinning or corrosion and map that condition back to us—all while the oil is in the tank."[4]

Group Effort

As was the case with OTIS, electrical engineers work with engineers from different disciplines to solve problems. Each engineer brings his or her own expertise to a project, which means everyone plays a role much like actors in a play.

For example, Roman's job as an electrical engineer was to provide the necessary power to bring his robots to life and allow them to successfully perform their tasks. With Rover, Scavenger, and OTIS, Roman decided to use a tether, which is like a cord or leash, to send power from him to the robots. The tether could also be used as a leash to retrieve the robots should anything go wrong.

Yet while an electrical engineer is in charge of controlling the power sent to a robot, a mechanical engineer designs the actual machinery and moving parts of a robot. Roman worked with a mechanical engineer to understand how much energy OTIS would need to use its ultrasonic equipment and swim through one million gallons of thick oil, forty to sixty feet deep.

Before a robot can move, it has to understand instructions, which requires electronic communications using a computer software program. With OTIS, Roman had to confer with a computer engineer on the team to discuss the best way to transfer information between them and the robot using the least amount of power.

Harnessing Nature

Electrical engineers often use their knowledge to transform natural-ly occurring forces, such as radio waves, into practical technology. Such is the case in the telecommunications industry, which employs tens of thousands of electrical engineers. One area of specialty with-in telecommunications that is growing rapidly right now is wireless

Electrical Engineering Spawns Computer Engineering

One of the main reasons electrical engineering is so important is the continuing tremendous growth of computer technology. In fact, until recently, the majority of professionals in the com-puter industry were electrical engineers. The growth was so substantial that the electrical engineering field sprouted a new engineering discipline called computer engineering, which is closely related to computer science.

According to Raymond B. Landis, an engineer and the author of *Studying Engineering: A Road Map to a Rewarding Career*, there is plenty of overlap between computer science and computer engineering, but in general, computer scientists focus primarily on software, while computer engineers work on hardware: "Some [computer engineers] work on the design of computer architecture in order to produce faster, more efficient computer systems. Others work on the design and development of electronic systems that enhance the ability of computers to communicate with other computers."

Computer engineering is growing so rapidly that it will prob-ably eclipse electrical engineering as the most populated engi-neering discipline. According to the Engineering Workforce Commission of the American Association of Engineering Societies, computer engineering was the fourth largest engineer-ing discipline in terms of Bachelor of Science degrees awarded in 1999, and makes up 11.6 percent of total engineering degrees. In that same year, the average salary for computer engineering graduates was $45,666. In this computer-oriented world, it is easy to see how computer engineering may easily surpass all other disciplines.

communications, which relies on invisible radio waves traveling through the air at the speed of light.

Larry Greenstein, electrical engineer and wireless communications expert, discusses his childhood fascination with electromagnetic waves: "When I was a boy, I knew there were electromagnetic waves in the air, but I didn't have a clue about the laws of physics and mathematics that explained them. I wanted to find out how electromagnetic waves, like those that come from the sun 93 million miles away, could be used to improve communications."[5]

Radio theory explains how electricity and magnetism combine to create a radio wave that can actually travel through space from one point to another. About forty years ago when Greenstein began to realize that he could have a career in communications, the use of radio to carry telephone calls was relatively new. Back then telephone calls traveled mostly over copper wires or coaxial cables, not through thin air. Today, the electromagnetic waves that intrigued Greenstein as a student are used to carry many millions of conversations around the world every day. The key technologies used for doing this are microwave radio and—even more widely used—optical fibers, which carry another kind of electromagnetic wave—light. Additional electromagnetic wave applications include X-rays, lasers (used in both fiber optics and medicine), and radiation therapies, all of which require the expertise of electrical engineers.

Harry Roman, the electrical engineer who developed the robots that now clean oil tanks and nuclear reactors all over the world, is also challenged with coming up with ways to harness the forces of nature for technological purposes. His latest project involves turning solar power from the sun into an energy source here on earth. Using his knowledge of mathematics, Roman converts sunlight into electricity with the help of solar panels, the black, domino-like structures found on the rooftops of some homes and buildings.

Mathematical Calculations

An electrical engineer must master many academic subjects, but none is applied more often than mathematics. For example, mathematical calculations were useful to Roman when he had to figure out how much power OTIS the robot would need to inspect oil tanks.

This required calculating OTIS's power consumption per minute and determining how many minutes OTIS would be in the tank. Roman explains the necessity of calculating power in robotics:

> Power is largely dependent on how much energy, expressed in kilowatt-hours, you would like to expend for a certain task, kind of like how we burn calories of food when we exercise. An electrical engineer working in robotics has to know how many kilowatt-hours a robot without a power cord requires before it runs out of power and stops just like a human does when he or she gets hungry.[6]

Roman used geometry to determine how OTIS needed to move around in dark oil where it is easy to get lost. Roman's team also relied on a radio beacon from outside the tank to locate OTIS within the tank, a technology sim-

A doctor views a patient's X-rays, images of the skeleton produced by photographing electromagnetic waves.

ilar to sonar used by submarines beneath the ocean.

Geometry also comes in handy when studying solar power because it helps electrical engineers understand the earth's astronomical movement around the sun during the day. Roman explains:

> I can tell you about how much energy comes from the sun each day and I can tell you realistically how much of that energy can be used by someone on the earth. I look at the time the sun starts hitting a panel at 8 A.M. in the summer to perhaps 4 or 5 P.M. in the afternoon. I'd be interested in calculating how much energy is coming down from the sky

and how that energy would be made available to a home that is equipped with a solar panel or a system of solar panels on it.[7]

Solar energy and robotics, however, were not Roman's first responsibility as a young electrical engineer in the power industry.

A Lightning Start

Usually young electrical engineers looking to work in the power industry will design power systems such as motors, generators, and the power transmission systems mounted on pole lines. Harry Roman explains how he began his career in the power industry: "I was involved in designing substations, switching stations, and analyzing the power flows of the network, what we call 'stock and trade' engineering. It's a traditional rite of passage for a new power engineer to design everything from a pole circuit to a transformer, but eventually you begin to work on more complicated projects."[8]

An example of a low-level design job in the energy field might be designing a pole line for distributing electrical power to a neighborhood of houses. If a new home is added to that neighborhood, the electrical engineer would determine how much additional power would be required to support the new home, which is known as load growth, a situation similar to plugging more and more appliances within a home to a single outlet.

New power engineers might also decide where to locate lightning arresters atop poles in areas that experience numerous electrical storms. A lightning arrester reroutes the sudden power surge caused by a lightning strike, which could cause a circuit to blow and create a blackout. In order for lightning arresters to work, electrical engineers must go on-site to make sure that they are properly installed.

Traveling in the Field

It is very common for electrical engineers to leave their offices and do work out in the field. For example, Roman frequently inspects other facilities and equipment. He may have to check his laboratory where solar panel systems are being tested or to inspect buildings currently using solar panel systems. Roman explains,

In my laboratory where I have systems being tested, I take a look at their performance to check on how well they are holding up in the real weather conditions to determine if the system is degrading because of all the wind and the rain and the snow and the sunlight. In the buildings where solar panel systems are up and running, I might check out the installations to see how well they have performed, which means getting out on the rooftops.[9]

Because solar panels reside on rooftops, they are vulnerable to harsh climates that can cause physical damage. For example, hail can break the glass of a solar panel or rain can leave a residue on the glass, hampering the solar panel's performance. Also, the sun itself can fade the color of the solar panels, which affects their ability to absorb sunlight being transformed into energy within the cell. As an electrical engineer, Roman makes sure that the system within the solar panel can function at its highest capacity.

Solar panels on a rooftop convert the sun's energy into electricity. These sensitive devices require the expertise of electrical engineers to ensure their optimum performance.

In addition to venturing beyond their offices, electrical engineers may also find themselves traveling around the country and the world to conferences or meetings with other engineers. These meetings are important because they provide opportunities for electrical engineers to brainstorm with other electrical engineers from all over the world to solve the challenging problems that will confront them in the future.

Future Challenges

In the coming years, electrical engineers will be responsible for tackling the most difficult technological problems. With the popularity of wireless communications devices like mobile phones, laptop computers, pagers, and personal digital assistants, electrical engineers are now challenged to improve voice quality and increase the speed at which data such as e-mail, pictures, and video can travel over wireless networks. Greenstein explains why consumers are looking for better wireless technology:

> More than ever people are moving around, so being reachable by cell phone has become very popular, and in some cases a necessity. Now we want to be able to take our computers with us too, so we can send and receive e-mails and browse the Web wherever we are, which means making wireless laptops and cell phones that function like mini desktop computers a reality.[10]

If wireless bandwidth can be vastly increased, people will be able to share high-quality video and experience high-speed access to the Internet without having to plug in electrical cords. According to Larry Greenstein, electrical engineers working in wireless telecommunications will be confronted by this challenge for the next twenty years, if not longer.

As for future electrical engineers working in the energy industry, increasing demands for electrical power will continue to be a challenge. These engineers will design and operate highly complex utility plants and power networks. As such engineers search for new ways to provide more power they will have to balance important economic and environmental issues. For example, switching to new energy sources might hurt the economy in the short term, but relying on fossil fuels such as petroleum could damage the environment in the long term.

What to Study

A student must tackle some of the most challenging courses in college to become an electrical engineer, one who works on old and new energy problems in the power industry or on the design and development of wired and wireless networks. As in all engineering disciplines, mathematics and the basic sciences provide the ideal foundation for electrical engineering study. College electrical engineering courses build on the math and science knowledge gained in high school by developing creativity and engineering skills. Related courses in computer science are also essential.

Other useful courses come from different disciplines such as mechanical engineering, materials science, manufacturing, management, and finance. As electrical engineering students progress, they take more advanced electrical engineering courses to prepare for

An engineer performs maintenance at an electrical substation. Electrical engineers design systems to generate electricity.

Earn While You Learn

An electrical engineering graduate with engineering work-related experience will certainly be more appealing to an employer compared with another candidate without such experience. One way to get this valuable experience is through cooperative education.

Cooperative education, offered through colleges and universities, requires that students alternate their academic study with work experience for a defined period of time. Some programs may require the student to work part-time and take academic courses part-time, while the more traditional types of programs may require six months of full-time study and six months of full-time work experience.

Besides the bonus of having practical experience in a field of study upon graduation, there are other benefits of cooperative education. An obvious one is the opportunity to earn money to pay for college expenses. In addition, although it may take longer for a student to graduate because of the extra time spent in cooperative education, cooperative learning experiences may decrease the time it takes to find a job later on because of the valuable contacts made during the program.

Each university handles cooperative education differently. For example, some universities consider cooperative education a mandatory part of their engineering programs, but at most institutions it is the choice of the students. Some universities offer academic credit, while other universities do not. Another variation exists in the amount of participation the university will have in a student's co-op experience. At those universities with a mandatory policy, many resources are available to the student, including a well-staffed office that finds co-op positions and then identifies the right student for the job. At the other end of the spectrum, students find their own program. In any event, cooperative education helps students develop professional, technical, and social skills, make network contacts, and better understand their interests and goals.

specialties such as computers, electronics, controls and robotics, power and energy, and telecommunications. For example, electrical engineering students who plan to work in telecommunications will find that courses on the basic laws of signal processing and radio engineering are essential.

Where to Study

As the most populated field of engineering, electrical engineering also has the highest number of schools offering the subject as a college major. High school graduates with a strong interest in a particular field may want to focus their attention on colleges located in parts of the country most closely associated with that field. For example, Silicon Valley, near San Francisco, is home to some of the best known computer, Internet, and semiconductor companies. These companies and others recruit electrical engineers from schools in this region.

Although telecommunications experts are in demand everywhere, the Northeast has several major companies. College students can benefit from electrical engineering programs and work opportunities closely tied to these and other companies.

Another region where electrical engineers are in demand is the Southwest. Texas has quickly become a state known for developing electronic equipment and data networking systems. For those who have no idea what they would like to focus on, there is plenty of time to learn, and with electrical engineering there are also plenty of places to learn.

Joining the Ranks

Companies from a wide variety of industries demanding people with high-tech skills will continue to seek skilled electrical engineers, which means that electrical engineering graduates have a strong chance of finding employment. According to a report from the National Association of Colleges and Employers, electrical equipment and computer manufacturers as well as engineering services firms showed the greatest interest in those students graduating with electrical engineering degrees.

According to the *Occupational Outlook Handbook*, a publication of the U.S. Bureau of Labor Statistics, electrical and electronics engineers held about 288,000 jobs in 2000, making their occupation the largest branch of engineering.

Most electrical engineering jobs are in engineering and business consulting firms; electrical and electronic equipment manufacturing; the design, development, and maintenance of industrial machinery and professional and scientific instruments; and the government. Other types of companies that rely heavily on electrical engineers include communications and utilities firms, manufacturers of aircraft and guided missiles, and computer and data processing services firms. More than one-third of all electrical and electronics engineers work in California, Texas, New York, and New Jersey, states where large electronics and telecommunications firms are concentrated.

Another area that constantly demands electrical engineers is national defense. There are numerous opportunities for those who want to work for companies that upgrade aircraft and weapons systems through improved navigation, control, guidance, and targeting systems.

Finally, for those who are interested in research and up to pursuing a doctoral program, promising careers await in the universities. There, one can conduct research and help to educate coming generations of electrical engineers.

Salary and Career Outlook

The large number of working electrical engineers has not lowered the profession's earnings potential. According to the July 2001 *Salary Survey*, a survey conducted four times a year by the National Association of Colleges and Employers, engineering graduates continue to receive high starting salaries. For example, the average starting salary for electrical engineering graduates was $51,910, a 7 percent gain over the previous year's estimate.

Young electrical engineers are more likely to earn a higher salary by working for a large company (greater than five hundred employees) rather than a small company. An exception is those engineers who work for small consulting firms with fewer than ten employees, but such firms usually hire electrical engineers with a lot of experience.

According to the *Occupational Outlook Handbook*, the median figure for annual earnings of electrical engineers was $64,910 in 2000. The lowest 10 percent earned less than $41,740, and the highest 10 percent earned more than $94,490. The median annual earnings in the industries employing the largest numbers

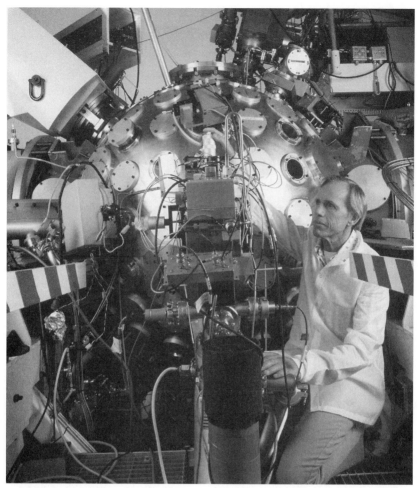

Electrical engineers may work in research laboratories that use sophisticated machinery such as the Nova laser (pictured), an extremely powerful X-ray laser.

of electrical engineers in 2000 was $69,700 for computer and office equipment; $67,570 for measuring and controlling devices; $65,830 for electronic components and accessories; $67,330 for search and navigation equipment; and $65,040 for engineering and architectural services.

In 1997 salaries for electrical and computer engineers were especially good at companies specializing in computer hardware and software, communications, and aerospace, but demand will change over time. For example, aerospace is a sector that can pay well but is subject to layoffs when the economy weakens.

The number of jobs available for electrical and electronics engineers will grow faster than the average for all occupations through 2010. Increased demand for electrical and electronics goods, especially advanced communications equipment, defense-related electronic equipment, and consumer electronics products, is the main reason why continued growth is expected. As electronics manufacturers dedicate large budgets to research and development, they will seek qualified electrical engineers familiar with the latest technologies to lead efforts to help them maintain a scientific edge against competitors.

It is not easy to become an electrical engineer. In fact, it is a challenging career filled with complex technical problems involving machinery, energy, and communications. But the best electrical engineers learn how to transform problems into progress, which brings power to the powerless and connects the disconnected.

Chapter 2

Mechanical Engineering: Making Mechanical Marvels

Electrical engineers make machines move, but it is mechanical engineers who make the machines. In fact, mechanical engineers also make the tools that make the machines, as well as the tools that make the tools. These men and women are responsible for the production of virtually every consumer product bought and sold every day all over the world.

As the second largest and one of the oldest engineering disciplines, mechanical engineering has become critically important to every industry. Its importance has resulted in the evolution of a wide variety of career opportunities ranging from engine building and heating and refrigeration, to manufacturing and product testing, to just about every industry here on Earth as well as beyond Earth, namely aeronautics and the space program. According to Raymond B. Landis,

Mechanical engineers design tools, engines, machines, and other mechanical equipment. They design and develop

Mechanical engineers at Ford Motors designed the world's first hydrogen-fueled internal combustion engine.

power-producing machines such as internal combustion engines, steam and gas turbines, and jet and rocket engines. They also design and develop power-using machines such as refrigeration and air-conditioning equipment, robots, machine tools, materials handling systems, and industrial production equipment.[11]

The work of mechanical engineers varies by industry and function. The American Society of Mechanical Engineers (ASME) lists thirty-six technical divisions, including applied mechanics; computer-aided design (CAD) and manufacturing; energy systems; and heating, refrigeration, and air-conditioning systems. ASME also lists eight technical committees, but to generally categorize the field, it is easiest to classify mechanical engineers into one of three fields: manufacturing (making a product using raw materials, which requires the building of the machines, tools, and manufacturing processes to accomplish this); energy (the production and transfer of energy);

and structures and motion in mechanical systems (the design of machines such as automobiles, milling machines, copying machines, and medical equipment).

Making It Right

Mechanical engineers are responsible for improving the way products are made. They think of ways to convert raw materials into end products. From start to finish, using a variety of equipment, machinery, and tools, mechanical engineers design manufacturing processes, often including automation and robotics, to help make the production of manufactured goods as efficient, cost-effective, and reliable as possible. For example, ordinary items such as rubber bands do not grow on trees. While rubber, the raw material from which they are made, comes from trees, rubber bands are ultimately created by mechanical engineers. Mechanical engineer Sherita Ceasar explains:

> When you go back into the manufacturing process behind even the simplest of items like rubber bands, you'll always find a mechanical engineer because there is a machine element in the raw material production of it. The machines that cut the rubber band into their various sizes and the machines that may be used to carry the material of rubber were built by mechanical engineers.[12]

A rubber band is an example of a finished product manufactured by mechanical engineers. Yet mechanical engineers also develop products that are components of larger products, which are then assembled by other companies or by consumers. For example, when a parent unpacks a child's bicycle, he or she follows directions created by mechanical engineers because it is they who designed the bicycle from the handlebars to the wheels to the holes in the frame into which screws are inserted. Moreover, mechanical engineers also create the screws, according to Ceasar, who spent a whole year in college on a project that focused on drawing a single screw thread.

The Need for Speed

Mechanical engineers build manufacturing equipment found on factory assembly lines that can churn out products in bulk at rates that no single human could match in terms of speed and precision. There are many professions that produce things, but it is mechanical engineers who make mass production possible. Carpenters, auto mechanics, and artists such as sculptors build and repair things every day; however, they usually work on one project at a time.

The distinction between a mechanical engineer and a craftsman is important. For example, a sculptor can make clay pot after clay pot, but a mechanical engineer can design machines and equipment that can produce hundreds of clay pots one hundred times faster than an individual sculptor. While a handmade clay pot is usually more valuable than many made by a machine, the machine-made pots will generate great value for the company that produces them. Mass production creates what is known as economies of scale, which means that it is a lot less expensive to set up a mechanical system to produce thousands of the same item than it is to produce a few of them by hand.

The public benefits, too, because items produced by companies that employ mechanical engineers are generally much less expensive than items built by hand. By making affordable products mechanical engineers improve the quality of life of billions of people.

The Engine Engineers

Mechanical engineers design products that change the lives of everyone. For example, the product that has done more to improve the way people live, work, and play is the automobile. Mechanical engineers are responsible for the basic internal combustion engine and all aspects of automotive manufacturing. More recently they are taking the lead in improving engine performance with respect to safety and the environment. Automotive engineers, a group that is part of the technical division within mechanical engineering that specializes in engine manufacturing, are constantly refining car engines. For example, the International Federation of Automotive Engineering Societies (FISITA), an independent world body representing over 167,000 automotive engineers in thirty-three countries, helps to create efficient, affordable, safe, and sustainable automotive transportation.

Today cars use less fuel, emit far less pollution, and are much safer than they were in the past. Automotive engineers have refined engines so that harmful emissions such as hydrocarbons and carbon monoxide have been dramatically reduced. For example, in the 1960s damaging exhaust emissions were in the range of one to three hundred parts per million (ppm). In the year 2000 emission concentrations were set to be in the range of five to sixty-five ppm, a 98 percent reduction.

Additionally, automotive engineers have developed a superior way to recycle cars so that now more than 80 percent of a vehicle—from fluids to batteries to tires to radios to practically every engine component—is recyclable. Work is underway to make use of even the remaining 20 percent after the car frame has been crushed and shredded. As for safety, automotive engineers are behind the latest mechanical advancements that protect human life on the roads, including safety belts, air bags, and stronger body frames.

Mechanical Medical Marvels

The desire of mechanical engineers to keep people safe and healthy is also evident in the medical world, where they have had

Robotic arms weld automobile chassis in an assembly line. The robotized assembly process produces cars efficiently and cheaply.

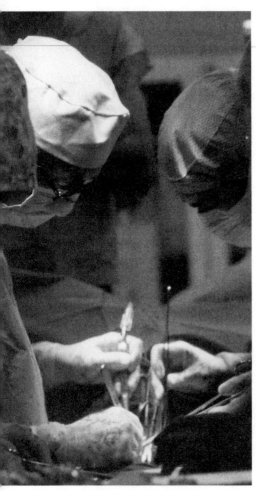

A team of doctors performs a heart-lung transplant. Mechanical engineers design the equipment to make such operations possible.

an incredible impact as designers of medical devices and systems. Saving time on an assembly line through an upgraded machine certainly helps business boom, but saving time in a hospital operating room can literally save human lives. For example, the collaboration of a unique team of mechanical engineers from Duke University Medical Center and a radiator division of General Motors developed the first commercial human-blood heat exchanger. This landmark device developed in 1957 permits a patient's body temperature to be safely and rapidly lowered to any desired and precisely controlled hypothermic level during open-heart surgery. It also allows for rapid rewarming at the conclusion of an operation. Prior to the human-blood heat exchanger, hypothermic surgery required several hours of hard-to-control, external emersion cooling before an operation and time to establish rewarming after an operation.

Mechanical engineers are also instrumental in providing bridges to organ transplants, that is, giving a patient who is waiting for an organ donor a chance to survive in the interim. Unfortunately many people die waiting for viable organs that can save their lives. According to the United Network for Organ Sharing in 2000, less than twenty-three thousand organs were available for seventy-four thousand people on transplant lists. One of the most critical situations involves people needing lung transplants, with the waiting time tripled to almost two years during the 1990s. According to *Red*

Herring magazine, a business magazine with a focus on new technologies, "the lack of a long-term alternative to lung transplantation condemns hundreds of thousands of people in the United States alone to slow and agonizing deaths."[13] Mechanical engineers and other health professionals are working right now to help such individuals by developing devices such as mechanical lungs that may be able to sustain a patient until a donor is available.

Joy Rides

While some mechanical engineers work on machines that help keep people alive, other mechanical engineers make machines for entertainment purposes, such as roller coasters. In amusement park ride design and development, the mechanical engineer is the technical manager of the project because the backbone of the ride system is purely mechanical.

Mark Hanlon, owner of Hanlon Engineering, has been integrally involved with the design and construction of more than fifty major amusement attractions, including Pirates of the Caribbean at Euro Disney in Paris. He describes the experience he and others created for passengers:

> Pirates take guests from a peaceful lagoon through a rush of water four stories high up a roller coaster–style chain ramp. From there, the boat is dumped into a pirate prison, complete with decaying bones before being dropped down a three-story-high waterfall. But the fall is only half of the story because at the bottom, the boat is surrounded by a giant wave of water that threatens to soak all aboard and swamp the boat. But "nay," all emerge damp from the mist, but otherwise dry.[14]

According to Hanlon, the Pirate ride then turns into a pirate show as passengers find themselves floating between two battling pirate ships with cannonballs flying everywhere and some of them landing dangerously near the boat. Eventually, the ride concludes with a final drop down a second waterfall into a huge cavern filled with treasure.

In order to construct such a wondrous fantasy experience, Hanlon describes how he worked with a team of engineers from start to finish:

The engineers started with a "kick-off meeting" where we openly discuss the technical challenges in creating the ride experience. With Pirates we were faced with many obstacles from designing a new larger and heavier boat to the up ramp, which could safely lift three boats at a time up the four-story ramp. Obviously, water management was critical because there is more water on the upper two levels than the lower level can hold, so automatic dams were designed for the top of each down ramp.[15]

Hanlon and the other engineers also had to use their engineering skills to calculate the ride capacity in mathematical terms of guests per hour, boat size, water depth, flume size, and the length of the ride.

Space Shuttle and Stealth Bomber

Mechanical engineers make sure that the machines they create can withstand external forces such as excessive heat. This becomes especially important for machines made for national defense and space exploration. The stealth bomber is just one example of a significant military aircraft that could not have been made without mechanical engineers. In fact, practically every weapon, vehicle, and piece of equipment used by the army, navy, and air force is created by mechanical engineers.

While working for a company that fulfilled military equipment contracts with the U.S. government, Sherita Ceasar contributed to the development of power supply components for the stealth bomber. She was responsible for the mechanical packing of the electronic circuit boards that controlled power and countermeasure devices for the stealth bomber.

Ceasar recalls, "I ensured that external forces such as extreme temperatures and vibration would not influence the assembly of the electronic components on that circuit board. Mechanical engineers must check all factors that could damage the way a mechanical product works, including acceleration, velocity, distance, and pressure."[16]

Similar concerns are confronted by mechanical engineers working on spacecraft. Astronaut and mechanical engineer Bonnie Dunbar began her professional career with a company that produced the tiles that made up the outer shell of the space shuttle. "I used my engineering skills to do the numeric analysis and the strength tests to ensure that the tiles did not melt at temperatures as high as 2300 degrees Fahrenheit. The space shuttle is designed to be reusable so its tiles must not wear away within different atmospheres."[17]

Dunbar and her associates used different types of heat to simulate the earth's atmosphere and the hotness of prolonged sunlight. "We wanted to determine how long it took for that heat to get back to the structure of the shuttle. I analyzed the equipment to find out

Astronomical Ambitions

The National Aeronautics and Space Administration, also known as NASA, depends upon mechanical engineers. In fact, about two-thirds of all astronauts in the space program have engineering degrees and all pilots on space flights have engineering degrees, according to Bonnie Dunbar, who has orbited the earth many times on several space shuttle missions.

In a personal interview, Dunbar explained why engineers are usually great decision makers in space: "Space travel is not very forgiving about opinion. Two plus two equals four. You may hold the opinion that it is three, but unfortunately that won't help you build a spacecraft. You've got to be right, and engineers from all disciplines insist on being right. It's that process of logic and being able to evaluate a situation and coming up with the correct answers that helps engineers become great astronauts."

Mechanical engineers need to be right about countless tasks they perform in the space program, which includes knowing how to make and fix structures and equipment. During one space shuttle flight, Dunbar was responsible for operating a mechanical arm that retrieved samples from space for testing and fixed existing equipment such as satellites orbiting the earth. On an upcoming space shuttle mission, that same robotic arm will be working on the famous Hubble telescope in deep space. Dunbar reveals, "The crew will spend a couple of days rendezvousing with the Hubble space telescope, capturing it with the robotic arm, and bringing it into the base for an analysis. The team will also be putting some new hardware on the Hubble space telescope."

The space shuttle crashes into a concrete wall during a test to determine how great an impact the ship can withstand. Such testing is supervised by mechanical engineers.

why certain processes weren't working properly and I had to help design devices to produce tiles that would be able to take the heat, as well as other external forces."[18]

Testing 1 . . . 2 . . . 3 . . .

In addition to making products, mechanical engineers are chiefly responsible for testing products. For example, Sherita Ceasar knows all about product testing from her days with a company that provided independent, impartial testing of commercial products. In that laboratory she tested everything from microwave ovens to ski goggles.

Ceasar recalled having a lot of fun conducting tests for microwave radiation leaks. "I had to produce destructive mechanism testing to ensure that microwave ovens didn't have any radiation leaks. I analyzed six different models with various different destructive tests, which included throwing lead balls at them, breaking spoons in the doors, dropping them, and crushing them."[19] While to some it might seem comical to destroy microwaves, the importance of such tests is clear to see. Radiation leaks could cause health problems and the manufacturers of microwave ovens as well as people who use microwave ovens need to be sure that the products would not be dangerous.

As for the ski goggles test, the only one in danger was Ceasar's mechanical dummy that wore the goggles. "We were testing fog resistance, so I put the ski goggles on the dummy and put the dummy in a refrigerator, generated a lot of steam in the refrigerator, and timed the dissipation of steam across the lenses of the goggles."[20]

Currently, Ceasar works in the telecommunications industry, specifically designing, developing, and testing pagers. Electrical engineers may be the architects behind the networks by which voice signals travel from one point to another, but the devices people use to talk and listen to one another during those conversations are made by mechanical engineers. Telephones, fax machines, and pagers are built by mechanical engineers like Sherita Ceasar, who speaks of the role of mechanical engineers in the telecommunications industry:

> The entire design of the pager comes from mechanical engineers. The plastics, the buttons, the printed circuit board within the pager, not to mention the basic elements that hold the pager together—the fasteners and the clips, even the screw that holds the battery door on the back of the pager to keep the electronics from being exposed. Then once it's built, mechanical engineers make sure that the pager can withstand its environment by testing it, which means dropping it, heating it, and freezing it.[21]

Ingenuity and Resourcefulness

Building and testing products are what mechanical engineers are known for, but many times it is their ability to fix malfunctioning equipment and solve difficult problems quickly that truly sets them apart. A great example of this occurs in a scene from *Apollo 13*, the film about NASA's efforts to save three astronauts stranded in space. A bag of tubes and random machine parts representing the only materials available on *Apollo 13* is dropped on a table. A team of engineers is then challenged to make a device out of the materials to generate breathable air within *Apollo 13* before its three astronauts suffocate. With limited resources and limited time, the engineers come through, and the rescue mission succeeds.

According to mechanical engineer and astronaut Bonnie Dunbar, "You can't test for everything on the ground. You'll always have a few surprises when you are in orbit. Each day we have a script to follow, but every day can be different. I've had to fix equipment on board and reprogram computers. Part of our training is being able to recognize unexpected, important events."[22]

The *Apollo 13* story and Dunbar's experiences illustrate two of the most important characteristics of mechanical engineers: ingenuity and resourcefulness. In short, they know how to come up with solutions to seemingly impossible problems, sometimes with little time and few tools.

Future Opportunities on Mars

One seemingly impossible problem currently confronting mechanical engineers working in the space industry is figuring out how to complete the first successful mission to Mars. With current technology, it takes six months to reach Mars, the closest planet to Earth.

Engineering Competitions

Local, regional, national, and international engineering and engineering-related competitions can provide students interested in mechanical engineering and other engineering disciplines some hands-on experience, while allowing them the chance to win trips or earn scholarship money. Many competitions allow for individual participation, but most require that students work in teams.

One competition is FIRST's (For Inspiration and Recognition of Science and Technology) Robotics Competition. One of the goals of the six-week annual robot design and build competition is to show high school students that the basic concepts of science, math, and engineering can be exciting.

The International Bridge Building Contest promotes the study and application of fundamental principles of physics, while giving students the opportunity to develop hands-on skills. The object of the contest is to see which student can design, construct, and test the most efficient bridge within the specifications.

Other competitions have required such feats as designing an engineering project useful to agriculture, modifying a sports utility vehicle to achieve increased fuel efficiency and near-zero emissions, designing and building a solar-powered boat, and creating a device that converts the gravity potential of water into mechanical power.

Obviously, the spacecraft and the space exploration equipment and gear used for moon launches and space shuttle trips will have to be radically changed in order to make it possible for people to arrive and survive on Mars.

Dunbar predicts that mechanical engineers will be part of the teams that come up with ways to use new lighter, yet stronger materials with which to build a Mars spacecraft. They will also be responsible for creating the equipment that will test the atmosphere and landscape of Mars. And, perhaps most important, mechanical engineers will design and develop the spacesuits that will keep astronauts alive on the Red Planet. Dunbar explains:

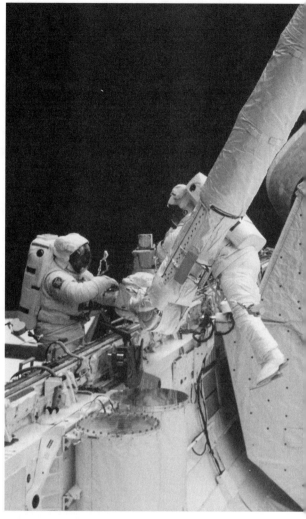

Astronauts operate equipment in space. Space travel would be impossible without the work of mechanical engineers.

The moon is a vacuum, and we know how to build spacesuits for vacuums. Mars has an atmosphere. We know there was once water there, and we have two meteorites picked up in Antarctica from Mars that show the potential start of microbial life. So the same system that we have designed for the moon will not work for Mars, which is probably the only planet in our solar system right now that you could walk on.[23]

So far only robots have touched the surface of Mars, and although that has been helpful, it is not the best way to retrieve information. After all, it is hard to operate robots on Mars from here on Earth where it takes forty minutes between each command. According to Dunbar, an astronaut possesses the best tool of all—the human brain. Building a spacesuit that can sustain human life on Mars is a top priority of mechanical engineers because it will offer a hands-on learning opportunity about Mars, which could have an incredible impact on the future of Earth.

Education

Students interested in studying mechanical engineering will find that there are nearly 250 accredited mechanical engineering programs in the United States. Mechanical engineering is a broad discipline, so it is best for students to choose a school that has a strong emphasis on the area in which they are most interested.

As previously mentioned, the numerous technical fields and subspecialties of mechanical engineering are generally grouped into three areas of study: energy, structures and motion in mechanical systems, and manufacturing. This translates into numerous areas of emphasis available at universities, such as automotives; heating, ventilating, and air-conditioning; materials science and engineering; computer-aided design and manufacturing; biomechanics and bioengineering; acoustics and vibration; and robotics.

Employment

Mechanical engineering graduates will find many opportunities upon graduation. According to the *Occupational Outlook Handbook*, there were approximately 221,000 employed mechanical engineers in 2000. More than half of these working mechanical engineers were in manufacturing, particularly in machinery, transportation equipment, electrical equipment, instruments, and fabricated metal products industries. The majority of the remaining employed engineers worked for engineering and management services, business services, and the federal government. Mechanical engineers will find that they can live wherever they choose since machines and mechanical systems can be found almost everywhere.

Employment of mechanical engineers is projected to grow about as fast as the average for all occupations through 2010. Overall manufacturing employment is expected to grow slowly, but not for mechanical engineers whose skills are needed in manufacturing as the demand for improved machinery and machine tools grows and industrial machinery and processes become more complex.

More job opportunities will also be available for mechanical engineering graduates in new areas of information technology and biotechnology. The emerging field of nanotechnology will also create new job opportunities for mechanical engineers. Another bright spot for graduates will be with business and engineering services firms as other industries continue to contract out to these firms to solve their engineering problems.

A mechanical engineer tests a vehicle designed to explore Mars. Space research is just one of many exciting fields open to mechanical engineers.

High Demand Means High Earnings

Mechanical engineers can expect to command competitive salaries. As reported by the *Occupational Outlook Handbook*, the median annual earnings of mechanical engineers was $58,710 in 2000, with the middle 50 percent earning between $47,600 and $72,850.

According to a 2001 salary survey by the National Association of Colleges and Employers, bachelor's degree candidates in mechanical engineering received starting offers averaging $48,426 a year; master's degree candidates had offers averaging $55,994; and Ph.D. candidates, $72,096.

Dream Machines

Perhaps more so than any other branch of engineering, the work of mechanical engineers is the easiest to recognize. The small devices people take for granted such as alarm clocks, toasters, electric toothbrushes, computers, and telephones are made by mechanical engineers. And so are the large devices—automobiles, airplanes, Ferris wheels, and elevators would not move, fly, and go up and down without mechanical engineers.

Compared with other engineering disciplines, the work of mechanical engineers is tangible. As Sherita Ceasar explains, "The

Aerospace Engineering

Orville and Wilbur Wright may have flown the first plane, but the airline industry would never have gotten off the ground without aerospace engineers. The same can be said for the space program. The Apollo flights, the space shuttle flights, and the countless satellites orbiting the earth could not leave the atmosphere if aerospace engineers did not do their jobs correctly.

As a technical division within mechanical engineering, aerospace engineers possess many of the same skills and interests as other mechanical engineers, but clearly their eyes are on the skies. According to Aprille Ericsson-Jackson in an online publication, *Graduating Engineer and Computer Careers Online*, "I wanted to work for an organization that put up satellites." Ericsson-Jackson realized this dream and now works as an aerospace engineer at NASA's Goddard Space Flight Center in the Guidance, Navigation and Control Center. At NASA, she has worked on a number of satellites, including XTE (X-Ray Timing Explorer) and TRMM (Tropical Rain Forest Measurement Mission).

Aerospace engineers are also critical to the military, as they design and develop military aircraft and missiles as well as defense systems. The specialties within aerospace engineering are aerodynamics, propulsion, thermodynamics, structures, celestial mechanics, acoustics, and guidance and control systems.

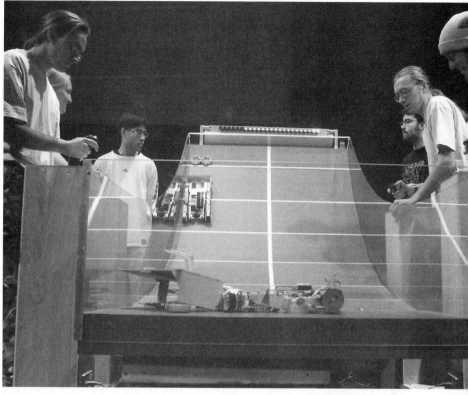

Two teams of mechanical engineers race the robots they have created. Mechanical engineers use their creativity and resourcefulness to create products that enhance the quality of life.

fun part of being a mechanical engineer is the ability to see an immediate impact on applying the science and theory to an actual product."[24] She first experienced that sense of wonder as a young girl, and mechanical engineering allowed her to have a career filled with the fun of discovery.

When Bonnie Dunbar was a young girl she dreamed of being an astronaut, and mechanical engineering helped her launch into space, "I think today's twelve-year-olds will be the ones that inspire us. They don't want to explore the same things we have explored — it's part of the human imagination."[25] In the future, mechanical engineers will continue to use their ingenuity and resourcefulness to make things of great value, and in the process improve life on this planet (and perhaps on other planets, too).

Chapter 3

Civil Engineering: Building Bridges, Tunnels, and More

What do the Golden Gate Bridge, the Empire State Building, the English Channel Tunnel, and the Hoover Dam have in common? These modern wonders could not be more different in size, shape, and structure, but they each share a common origin—the creative minds of civil engineers.

Civil engineering is the third largest and the oldest branch of engineering with major civil engineering projects dating back more than 5,000 years. Today, according to Raymond B. Landis, civil engineers "plan, design, and supervise the construction of facilities essential to modern life. Projects range from high-rise buildings to mass transit systems, from airports to water treatment plants, from space telescopes to off-shore drilling platforms."[26]

There are many different kinds of civil engineers. Structural engineers create stadiums, skyscrapers, bridges, and office buildings;

Environmental Engineering

Civil engineers who specialize in environmental engineering help to improve their communities. For years, buildings in Sussex County, New Jersey, discharged raw wastewater into the Walkill River, killing fish and turning the once clear stream into black rolling sludge. Fortunately, local environmental engineers such as Steve Donati built a wastewater collection system and wastewater treatment facility to keep raw sewage out of the Walkill River so that today it is clean again and the trout are back.

Donati became a licensed environmental engineer by passing an Engineer-in-Training exam, obtaining sufficient experience in the environment field, and then passing another exam to become a Professional Engineer. Donati spends a lot of his time not only cleaning polluted water, but advising clients how to tap into and dispose of water. In a personal interview with Donati he shared his views on water: "When you think about the basics of life, water is the most important element. Building a building is great, but without clean water, you're going nowhere."

For example, there are plans to construct a ski resort in a town near where Donati works. Local citizens fear that there will be a negative effect on the environment. To Donati the biggest obstacle to the project is water. "The proposed resort complete with luxury condos looks great on paper and will probably be beautiful when completed, but if they cannot bring enough water in and then properly treat wastewater, it could bring the entire multimillion-dollar project to its knees."

Environmental engineers like Donati are also responsible for controlling, preventing, and eliminating air and land pollution, which typically involves designing air quality control programs and landfills. Donati calls an improperly built landfill a "time bomb waiting to explode." Even the smallest of solid waste items such as batteries leach toxic chemicals such as mercury, which if not contained by a landfill liner will mix with other chemicals to form a "toxic soup" that eventually winds up in groundwater or in streams or lakes. "Bugs absorb the mercury, small fish eat the bugs, bigger fish eat the small fish, and the toxins multiply in a process called biomagnification," said Donati. "If we eat the toxic fish, then those chemicals are absorbed into our bodies—it's a nasty process."

transportation engineers move people and goods safely and efficiently, and design and maintain facilities such as highways and railroads; environmental engineers may be called on to provide safe drinking water or clean up sites contaminated with hazardous materials; water resources engineers are focused on the quality and quantity of water available and on protecting people and buildings from storm water; and construction engineers use their knowledge of construction, finance, and management to turn designs into structures.

These fields cover a wide range of projects and require unique capabilities, but in general the work performed by civil engineers may involve extensive hands-on field work, an element of danger, a solid knowledge of the earth's limited resources, adequate mathematical skills (particularly in geometry), and an ability to communicate with the public.

Building Bridges

Many civil engineering graduates will choose to work on a structure most often associated with civil engineers: bridges. Some bridges are awesome in size with multiple levels such as the George Washington Bridge in New York, while others are more modest, crossing small creeks or train tracks. Regardless, civil engineers are the experts when it comes to bridge building, an extremely complicated process requiring exceptional organizational skills, years of technical training, and lots of patience.

Ed Dauenheimer, a civil engineer who spent most of his career working with bridges, provides some insight into the process. First, the civil engineer needs to get information about the existing site, which means conducting surveys and reading maps. Then, according to Dauenheimer, with the civil engineer's supervision, information about the soil conditions below the ground surface is collected. "We drill holes into the ground to learn what's under the surface and decide if it can support the weight that the bridge will place on the ground."[27]

Based on the initial information, civil engineers will then develop a number of preliminary designs for the bridge, using computer-aided design (CAD) systems. From these designs, civil engineers decide on the location of the roadway that will go across the bridge and how high the bridge should be based on whether the bridge is spanning water or an existing roadway. According to Dauenheimer,

Once the basic parameters are established, structural engineers will set the configuration of the bridge based on the required opening and the existing ground conditions. The final design for the bridge involves determining the size and arrangement of the main bridge members which span the opening (superstructure) and those members which support the superstructure such as piers and abutments (substructure).[28]

Tackling Tunnels

In some cases, going under a body of water or through a mountain range is better than going over it, which means constructing tunnels, another area of expertise of civil engineers. Tunnels can be wide enough to accommodate humans traveling in cars and trains or more streamlined for power lines and water supplies. No mat-

New York City's George Washington Bridge bustles with traffic at night. Bridges are one of many structures that civil engineers design.

ter the purpose, tunnel building can be extremely challenging because to a great extent it involves conquering natural environments such as rivers, lakes, and oceans, as well as hard rock deep underground.

The obstacles faced by Walter Konon, a civil engineer specializing in tunnels, during the construction of the Roosevelt Island tunnel in New York show exactly how challenging tunnel construction can be. Konon explains, "The tunnel contains two subway track bores stacked on top of two railroad tracks running from Queens through Roosevelt Island and into Manhattan. It required blasting through the hard rock beneath Roosevelt Island and inserting a preassembled tube into a hole forty-five feet in diameter."[29] These preassembled tubes were actually built in Norfolk, Virginia, and floated up the Atlantic Coast by barge and lowered into the East River where Roosevelt Island is situated. The tubes, consisting of steel with concrete encasement with ballast pockets so they would sink, could only be lowered to the bottom of the East River during a brief one-hour window of opportunity because of currents and tidal effects.

As a civil engineer on that project, Konon was responsible for building a ventilation structure to supply air to the tunnels. He explains, "Because it was a transit tunnel, we needed to provide a fresh air system, unlike a water tunnel that would not have people in it."[30] He led a team that created a seventy-foot-long shaft to the surface where a ventilation building pumped in fresh air. Konon also worked with the teams that placed tons of crushed stone on the bottom of the East River bed to provide a level surface on which to drop the tubes and to hold the tunnel tubes in place securely against swift currents and rising tides.

Workers tighten bolts on the cast-iron lining of New York City's East Side tunnel. Tunnel workers carefully follow the plan designed by civil engineers.

Applying Mathematics

Civil engineers often use mathematical subjects such as geometry and trigonometry, which deal with dimensions and angles, to help them meet the challenge of building bridges and tunnels. For example, mathematical analyses help civil engineers figure out how much flexibility must be built into a bridge or skyscraper in order to withstand external factors such as wind, heat, and cold. Dauenheimer explains, "A bridge is a complicated three-dimensional structure. Since the geometry varies from one end of the bridge to the other the challenge for bridge engineers is to create a roadway on the bridge which is smooth to drive over."[31]

Geometric positioning is very basic to deciding on the best place to put a road or a bridge. Although civil engineers today rely on high-tech equipment like global positioning satellites for mapping and surveying purposes and computers for design work, a solid knowledge of geometry and trigonometry is still important. Civil engineering graduates will also find that basic mathematics also comes into play for tasks such as calculating how much weight a structure can take. For example, before loading a crane to lift and lower a heavy object into a tunnel, calculations must be made to determine where to position the crane, whether or not the crane can handle the weight, and that the object can fit through the tunnel opening.

But while mathematics is essential Konon says, "You don't have to win a Noble Prize in math to be a civil engineer. It's a false image that engineers sit at a computer and do calculations all day long. I'd say that 95 percent of your time is spent working with people, often on a job site. That means about 5 percent of your time involves hardcore mathematics."[32]

Working with Materials

Civil engineers use their knowledge of materials, such as stone, steel, concrete, wood, and asphalt, to ensure that a structure will last a long time, perhaps forever. Because civil engineers are aware of the earth's limited resources, they try to design facilities for long lives and low maintenance.

Depending on the type of project, decisions must be made as to which materials should be used to build bridges and tunnels. For example, not all rock is the same. Some types of rock might crack easily, which means that it will not make a good foundation for a fifty-story skyscraper, but it might suffice for a two-story single family home.

Konon explains, "Civil engineers analyze rock to make sure it can carry the load before a project starts. If the rock fractures it could cause shifting in the foundation of a bridge. I can't dig a hole fifty feet deep and then make a decision. These things are preplanned and someone needs to make an evaluation of what a particular rock can hold."[33]

Civil engineers must study the properties of steel, a building material commonly used as frames for buildings and bridges. Dauenheimer discusses some of the differences between steel and concrete: "A steel member can have the strength of thirty-six thousand pounds per square inch, whereas a concrete member might have the strength of five thousand pounds per square inch. In bridge construction, civil engineers evaluate how much of these materials are needed to safely carry the anticipated number of vehicles that will be on that bridge."[34]

Hands-On

As a group, civil engineers tend to enjoy working on a job site and very often have backgrounds that include experience as manual laborers and operators of construction equipment. According to Dauenheimer, the best civil engineers know construction from the ground up. "If someone has had experience in the field then that will help him or her become a better civil engineer. In fact, civil engineering is a career that combines field work with office work."[35]

Walter Konon shares Dauenheimer's opinion:

I like the idea of working with something real, something physical. I'm now in the construction area of civil engineering. I like the day-to-day process of building something because at the end of the day I have instant gratification. I know what went well and what didn't. I have worked on a lot of projects in the New York metropolitan area and I like driving by things I've worked on and showing my kids.[36]

Having hands-on experience not only makes some people better civil engineers, it inspires them to become civil engineers. Dauenheimer shares his work experience:

The Difference Between Architects and Civil Engineers

Civil engineers are often confused with architects. Although these professions are similar, and architects and civil engineers often collaborate on projects, there is a distinct difference between the two. According to Ed Dauenheimer in a personal interview, an architect "provides for the human function within a building." Therefore, an architect is the lead professional for commercial and residential facilities like office buildings and houses because the primary occupants of those structures are people.

Dauenheimer went on to explain, "In commercial or residential buildings there are a lot of human factors to consider: How will people get in and get out? How large does the workspace have to be? For heavy construction projects such as airports, sewage systems, highways, and bridges, a civil engineer is the lead professional because the 'occupants' are planes, vehicles, and vessels, not human beings."

Architects hire civil engineers, particularly structural engineers, to help them with their design. They also hire civil engineers to do the drainage and site design, things found outside the building. Furthermore, architects call on civil engineers when an existing building needs to be refurbished. For example, if an architect wants to expand floor space or change the function of the second floor of a building, a civil engineer will tell him or her how to do it from a structural perspective. So while architects and civil engineers may take some of the same courses in college, there is a big difference in training.

Before I became a civil engineer, I worked for a construction company that built a water tunnel. That's probably what got me interested in moving into the engineering area. It was a good experience taking part in the physical end of the business because I literally saw something come from nothing. That's the attraction of civil engineering, going from a concept to an actual facility, in this case a tunnel delivering water

A team of civil engineers inspects an Arkansas state bridge. Once structures are built, civil engineers carry the responsibility of inspecting them.

to the people of New York City. That's very rewarding.[37]

Passing Inspection

Once the monumental task of completing a bridge or a tunnel is accomplished, the civil engineer will then be responsible for inspecting it. Structures such as bridges and tunnels cannot be left unattended because of the wear and tear and exposure to weather conditions they endure on a daily basis. In fact, if a structure is not properly monitored it could lead to catastrophe.

Dauenheimer refers to a famous tragic event: "The biannual bridge inspection program became a mandate after the Silver Bridge disaster over the Ohio River in West Virginia." The collapse happened on December 15, 1967, at approximately 5:00 P.M. on a Friday evening and took the lives of forty-six people when thirty-one vehicles plunged into the water. Dauenheimer continues, "Now, if a bridge is located over a waterway, it must undergo a detailed underwater inspection every four years using scuba divers. During a bridge inspection, we are literally looking at the bridge for physical signs of potential damage, and civil engineers are the best professionals to conduct such inspections."[38]

Tunnels undergo similar scrutiny. According to Konon, who currently works in forensic engineering, a branch of civil engineering that investigates why structures weaken and collapse, "Once you build a tunnel, it deteriorates over time. Metal rusts, concrete cracks, water leaks occur. An earthquake might shake a tunnel and cause a crack."

Konon goes on to explain that in water tunnels, civil engineers will go inside the tunnel in boats, check for cracks or leaks, and decide whether or not repairs need to be made. "It's important to learn by our mistakes and analyze what went wrong and what could be done differently in the future so it doesn't happen again."[39]

Risky Business

Working with such strong materials as steel and stone high above and far below the earth means that civil engineering, to some extent, can be a dangerous profession. Konon explains,

> You try to make construction areas as safe as possible, but realistically you do have accidents and sometimes fatalities. To some extent that adds to the challenge. If you're going to be a research librarian you're going to be happy sitting behind a computer poring over volumes of information. If that's what you enjoy, that's great. Construction, on the other hand, sometimes places people in uncertain natural environments.[40]

Konon should know. After all, while building the Roosevelt Island tunnel, he spent months sixty to seventy feet beneath the surface of the earth. Konon shares his thoughts on this experience: "With tunneling you go where no one has gone before, because the rock has been there for millions of years of geologic time. I've always thought of it as a different world with beautiful mineral formations and crystals. When punching through rock, I even imagined discovering dinosaur eggs, maybe even Godzilla!"[41]

In order to get through rock, civil engineers work with explosives. Konon is a member of the International Society of Explosives Engineers, a group that uses explosives, promotes explosives safety, and measures vibrations from explosives to make sure that adjacent structures are not damaged. According to Konon, "Understanding explosives is part of civil engineering. Heavy construction projects such as roadways, dams, tunnels, and bridges often require rock to be blasted away to make room for foundations."[42]

Public Input

Managing explosives is one thing, but managing explosive public issues is another, and in both cases civil engineers play a part as they must interact with state and local governments, as well as the public. If there is one branch of engineering that is "political," it is civil engineering. The majority of projects requiring civil engineers are funded by the government, which means they are paid for with tax money. Typically, when there is a need for a new bridge, road, or tunnel, the responsible governing body will issue a request for proposal. In this case, civil engineering firms will submit competing proposals, and the contract is usually awarded to the lowest qualified bidder.

Civil engineering projects also require public approval before they can begin. For example, residents of a town may not be in favor of a new highway, so civil engineers might have to appear as representatives at municipal hearings to present their projects and explain why the new highway will be a benefit to the community. Facing such audiences could be more daunting than installing a highway. Dauenheimer discusses the relationship between the public and civil engineers: "We build things on public lands, not company property, so there is a need for public input. Civil engineers must be able to *sell* projects to people. That's the big difference between civil engineering and other engineering disciplines."[43]

Education

A student with aspirations of becoming a civil engineer should prepare with a well-rounded education that includes English, algebra, plane geometry, trigonometry, advanced mathematics, chemistry, physics, history, foreign language, and computer courses, according to the American Society of Civil Engineers.

Civil engineering candidates will find that hundreds of colleges offer accredited civil engineering programs. Most of these programs grant a bachelor's degree after four years of study. Others offer a program in which the student receives a bachelor's degree after four years of study and a master's degree after the fifth. According to the American Society of Civil Engineers, the first three years of a civil engineering program offer a solid foundation in science and introductory courses in all of the civil engineering technical areas, giving the student a sampling of all aspects of the field.

A World of Opportunities

After civil engineering students complete their studies, it is time to find the right place to use their skills. As reported by the *Occupational Outlook Handbook*, civil engineers held about 232,000 jobs in 2000.

Clouds of dirt and rock billow above a dynamite explosion at the site of the Hoover Dam. Civil engineers oversee construction of massive structures like the dam.

More than 50 percent of this number worked for consulting firms developing designs for new construction projects. Approximately one-third of the jobs were in federal, state, and local government agencies, with the remaining number working in construction and manufacturing industries. A large number of the twelve thousand self-employed civil engineers used their skills as consultants.

State and county governments employ civil engineers in a variety of agencies, such as the Department of Transportation, Department of Environmental Protection, and Department of Community Affairs. Towns also employ full-time civil engineers to oversee municipal public works projects, including the enforcement of local zoning laws, sewage collection, and map services.

Civil engineers usually work near major industrial and commercial centers, often at construction sites. Some projects are situated in

Professional Registration

Only about 30 percent of practicing engineers have achieved the designation of Professional Engineer, but that number is considerably higher for civil engineers because they are responsible for public safety.

For all engineers, the Professional Engineer credential—indicated by the letters P.E. after the engineer's name—is impressive and can open many doors for the engineer who has obtained it. Laws may vary from state to state, but four steps are typically required to become a Professional Engineer. The first step requires graduation from an ABET-accredited engineering program. The second step requires that the Fundamentals of Engineering (FE) examination be taken and passed. This eight-hour exam is offered twice a year, in April and October. The first four hours of this multiple-choice test cover topics common to all engineering disciplines, such as mathematics, chemistry, and basic engineering sciences. When this test is passed the student receives the title of Intern Engineer or Engineer-in-Training.

The next step requires four years of acceptable experience as an Intern Engineer. The next and final step to becoming a Professional Engineer can be accomplished by successful completion of the Principles and Practice of Engineering (PE) examination, an eight-hour exam offered twice a year, in April and October.

More information about the process of becoming a Professional Engineer is available at the website of the National Council of Examiners for Engineers and Surveyors (NCEES), www.ncees.org.

remote areas or in foreign countries. In some jobs, civil engineers move from place to place to work on different projects.

According to Dauenheimer, "If you are interested in civil engineering, you also should be interested in traveling. There are tremendous opportunities if you are willing to travel nationally and internationally."[44] He knows, as he began his career in West Germany providing data about military airfields throughout Europe while working with the U.S. Army Corps of Engineers. Another job with a construction management company based in New York City brought him to countries like Venezuela, Lebanon, Syria, Jamaica, and Puerto Rico. A sampling of his overseas projects include working with a Lebanese construction firm to develop a computerized construction management system and developing plans for a major coastal resort with a Venezuelan architectural firm.

Salary

Civil engineering students can expect to command competitive salaries. According to the *Occupational Outlook Handbook*, the median annual earnings of civil engineers in 2000 was $55,740, with the middle 50 percent earning between $45,150 and $69,470. The median annual earnings of civil engineers employed by the federal government was $63,530; the median earnings for state government was $54,630; and, for local government, $56,830.

According to a 2001 salary survey by the National Association of Colleges and Employers, bachelor's degree candidates in civil engineering received starting salary offers averaging $40,616 a year; master's degree candidates received an average offer of $44,080; and Ph.D. candidates, $62,280.

Engineering Civilization

Fortunately there will be ample job opportunities for civil engineers in the future. According to the *Occupational Outlook Handbook*, employment of civil engineers is expected to increase about as fast as the average for all occupations through 2010.

As the population increases, society will look toward civil engineers to design and build higher capacity transportation, water supply and pollution control systems, and large buildings and building complexes. It will also be the responsibility of civil engineers to fix or replace existing roads and bridges. Because the construction industry tends to be affected in times of economic slowdown, civil engineering opportunities in this field will also slow during these times.

While all fields of engineering, including civil engineering, help to advance business, civil engineers literally advance civilization. The roads they pave allow people to travel from city to city and state to state. The dams they construct bring power to thousands of people. And the bridges and tunnels they build connect points on maps that were previously disconnected, which helps to create unity among different cultures. In short, the large-scale projects of civil engineers help large segments of people—not just individuals or single companies, but communities.

The American Society of Civil Engineers summarizes the importance of civil engineers to society: "Civil engineers are problem solvers, meeting the challenges of pollution, traffic congestion, drinking water and energy needs, urban redevelopment, and community planning."[45] That is why governments pay for most of the work performed by civil engineers: Governments are responsible for improving relations among communities and stimulating economic progress. Fundamental to such advancements is a modern infrastructure

Civil Engineering Soldiers

The U.S. armed forces have a great history of defending the country from hostile, foreign enemies, but not all threats to the nation are human in nature. Actually, nature itself can be very threatening. For example, if a dam breaks, flooding a community, the army can not do much about it. But the U.S. Army Corps of Engineers (USACE) certainly can.

The corps has serviced the United States of America for more than two hundred years by providing engineering, construction, and water resources expertise. In doing this, they save lives, ease human suffering, and prevent property damage. For example, following a major flood or coastal storm the corps may assist the community by removing debris to allow important transportation routes to be reopened, clearing blockages of critical water supply intakes and sewer outfalls, and helping to restore critical public services or facilities. During circumstances in which a community has contaminated water supplies that represent a substantial threat to the public health, the corps may be responsible for getting and distributing bottled water, providing a temporary connection of a new supply to the existing system, or installing temporary filtration systems.

Civil engineering graduates looking to work with a major army command that provides relief to U.S. citizens during times of natural disasters or emergencies, and perhaps travel to do so, may find that the USACE is right for them.

A U.S. Army Corps of Engineers dredge passes beneath a bridge. The corps is comprised of civil engineers trained to respond to crises.

consisting of safe roads, bridges, dams, and tunnels. Yet it is not just highways and byways that make up a community. There are buildings, too, powered by electricity and flowing with potable water. Civil engineers are behind all these high-profile projects. Without their ability to spark progress continually and to improve the way people live, civilization would be at a standstill.

Chapter 4

Chemical Engineering: The Right Mix

All areas of engineering are challenging to master, but few are more challenging than chemical engineering. This is because chemistry, the core subject behind chemical engineering, involves complex scientific formulas and requires knowledge of basic elements and microscopic particles.

Yet unlike chemists, chemical engineers are less focused on pure chemistry than they are on the application of chemistry. Again, like engineers in other disciplines, chemical engineers are charged primarily with finding ways to put science and engineering principles to work to help corporations and organizations create useful, cost-effective products that will benefit consumers and result in business success. Chemical engineer Sandra Dudley states the difference between chemists and chemical engineers in simple terms: "Chemists ask the question: 'Can I make this material in a lab?' whereas chemical engineers ask: 'Can I put this material into practice?'"[46]

The efforts of chemical engineers are not always easy to recognize, yet they play a critical role in the production of practically every product consumed and touched every day. These professionals have a huge impact on the food people eat and the medicines they take. They sometimes work with dangerous chemicals, but their efforts to improve life on earth are felt by everyone.

A Hand in Everything

Basic items that people use every day such as plastics, building materials, food products, pharmaceuticals, synthetic rubber, synthetic fibers, and petroleum products such as shampoos, soaps, cosmetics, and shower curtains could not be created without the expertise of chemical engineers. According to Dudley,

> Chemical engineers have their hands in developing almost any material. Simple things like paper need chemical engineers, because creating paper is a very chemically intensive process. Scotch tape wouldn't be sticky without chemical engineers. And it's chemical engineers who determine the

A professor of chemical engineering proudly displays a sophisticated electron microscope. Chemical engineers identify practical applications for the science of chemistry.

right mix of chemicals that not only make purple paint purple, but make purple paint dry quickly, and adhere to walls without running.[47]

In the clothing industry, chemical engineers work to make clothing more comfortable, more durable, fire-retardant, or water-resistant. In the food industry, chemical engineers use their knowledge to improve the safety, nutrition, and desirability of food. Whether the demand is for low-fat, low-cholesterol, sugar-free, or microwave-safe products, a chemical engineer is hired to engineer products to meet these needs. In fact, in addition to making food, chemical engineers help grow it.

Cropping Up

Chemical engineers help develop products that protect crops from insects or help crops grow more quickly. For example, new and improved fertilizers have been made from a mixture of elements devised by chemical engineers.

While an employee at a fertilizer company in North Carolina, chemical engineer Stephanie Sullivan and her team worked to improve processes involving raw materials from that region and to develop a combination of chemicals to produce superior types of plant fertilizer. First, phosphate rock found underground in that region was strip-mined and transported to a chemical plant. Next, sulfur, a by-product of the crude oil refining process, was brought in by train to Sullivan's company where it underwent a chemical reaction to form sulfuric acid. Then the sulfuric acid was applied to the phosphate rock dug up from the mine to create phosphoric acid.

Sullivan's team at another chemical plant then blended phosphoric acid with ammonia in a tank, producing a binder solution, like a paste, that was then sprayed onto an existing bed of dry materials in a twenty-five-foot-long granulator. Each step in the process produced chemical reactions until at last diammonium phosphate, a solid granular fertilizer, was produced. Sullivan explains,

The goal was to more efficiently make a product that encouraged plant growth and helped make the plants grow better, and we were successful. My company sold fertilizer all over the world to places as far away as China. It was an interesting place to work as a chemical engineer and the end result was worthwhile because it ultimately helped feed people.[48]

Cure Givers

Another important way that chemical engineers help people is through their efforts in the research, development, and manufacture of medical products and medications. These products prevent diseases from harming and even killing people, and help people with chronic illnesses to have a better quality of life.

For example, some chemical engineers work as biomedical specialists in laboratories designing artificial organs such as hearts and lungs that can act as temporary replacements while donors are sought. Others may work in the biotechnology industry creating products such as antibiotics and insulin. Still others may help develop innovative materials to deliver medications such as the plastic capsules used for controlled release medications or transdermal medications that can be applied outside the body and absorbed through the skin.

Chemical engineers in the pharmaceutical industry ensure that each and every tablet or capsule is manufactured exactly the same way. Any mistakes made in the manufacturing process can cause a lot of damage financially to the company that produced the drug because they would have to throw away millions of tablets. And it would be tragic if a poorly manufactured drug went to market and people suffered as a result.

At the pharmaceutical company where Stephanie Sullivan now works, her team is responsible for the technical operations used in producing pharmaceutical tablets that combat asthma, high cholesterol, or high blood pressure. They manage the production of large batches of tablets that must be thoroughly tested at various stages in the manufacturing process to ensure that each and every tablet is of the utmost quality. An important part of Sullivan and her team's job is to design and conduct the necessary validation testing when, for example, it is desired to scale-up the process to make a larger batch of tablets. Testing is done to be sure that the manufacturing process of the larger batch produces the same quality product as that of the smaller batch. One of the tests used by Sullivan and her team simulates how the drug is absorbed in the human body by determining if the active ingredient dissolves from the tablet in the specified amount of time. According to Sullivan,

If something atypical occurs during the manufacturing process, we must determine what went wrong, the extent of the problem, and how it affects the product. A team of people, including chemical engineers like me, analyze the atypical event to ensure that the product has not been negatively affected. It's our call whether or not that product is released to the public. Our industry is strictly regulated by the Food and Drug Administration and we must document everything we do, from adding ingredients in making the tablets to testing samples of each batch produced before it goes to market. Teamwork, good manufacturing processes, and thorough tests are critical to ensure the safety and efficacy of any pharmaceutical product manufactured.[49]

Women in Engineering

One myth about engineering is that it is not a career for women. That notion, however, fades every year as more and more women prove that when it comes to the technical problems associated with engineering, it is solutions that matter, not gender.

Yet while women are as likely to graduate from college as men, they are less likely than men to choose science and engineering fields. The false belief that boys are naturally better at math than girls or that engineering is not a "feminine" pursuit may have a lot to do with that.

However, women are just as capable as men when it comes to engineering. Although fewer women are enrolled in engineering programs, the number of women enrolled in all undergraduate engineering programs increased every year from 1989 to 1997. And the percentage of women currently enrolled in chemical engineering programs is the highest of any other major engineering discipline. According to the American Institute of Chemical Engineers, 36 percent of chemical engineering undergraduate students are women. The Society of Women Engineers is an organization that works to dispel the myths that keep young girls from dreaming of becoming engineers by providing networking opportunities that will most likely continue to increase the number of women in engineering programs.

A chemical engineer monitors production of pharmaceuticals, ensuring that the medications are of the highest quality.

Quality Control

Similar to their work in the pharmaceutical industry, chemical engineers in other industries must confront and conquer the challenge of producing the same products in massive numbers, which means quality control is an extremely important task for many chemical engineers. Quality control is what makes Coca-Cola taste like Coca-Cola and wool sweaters feel like wool sweaters. Creating a chemical process that produces one type of product is one thing, but devising a process that can produce a batch of thousands or millions of the exact same product over and over presents many more technical challenges. According to Sandra Dudley,

> Any time you're looking to do something on a large scale, whether you're making soft drinks or baking bread, you must have a chemical engineer on hand to determine the quantities that need to be used and how long the process should last. For example, one day you might try a new brand of bubble gum and like it because it has just the right amount of sweetness, pops well, and chews well. But the next time you buy it, it's salty, mushy, and you can't blow a bubble. Well, that company has not employed a chemical engineer to ensure that the formula for the bubble gum is being used consistently. Perhaps the company is not manufacturing the

bubble gum at the right temperature or maybe they are cooking it too long or not enough. Chemical engineers fix such problems or prevent them from happening by using their knowledge of chemistry, physics, algebra, and calculus to make sure that a product is mass-manufactured the same way day in and day out.[50]

Preventing Pollution

Chemical engineers play a role in the prevention of pollution, an unfortunate by-product of mass manufacturing. In fact, chemical engineers are very active in the crusade to keep the environment clean. As reported by Raymond B. Landis, they are responsible for "creating ways to clean up problems of the past, preventing pollution in the future, and extending our shrinking natural resources."[51] Their efforts often lead to improvements in the environment because of the creation of cleaner manufacturing processes, cleaner fuels to power cars, and safer methods of disposing of industrial wastes.

Sandra Dudley encountered a challenge involving air emissions during one of her first assignments as a chemical engineer. Residents of a small town complained about an offensive odor coming from a nearby manufacturing facility. The company that owned the factory employed many of the people in the community, so simply shutting down the facility was not an option because it would have put people out of work. Yet it was clear that something had to be done about the "rotten egg smell" that was ruining the quality of life in the town. Dudley's team came up with a brilliant, natural solution using a biofiltration technique, which uses compost, pine bark, and mulch to degrade organic contaminants. According to Dudley, "Any manufacturing operation is going to have emissions, but companies that care about the environment will use technology to prevent their emissions from causing damage. In this case, we used biofiltration."[52] Dudley and her colleagues discovered that microorganisms living in mulch materials commonly found in gardens and lawns could change the particles responsible for the offensive emissions coming from the factory.

By setting up a system by which the "rotten egg" fumes could pass through a filter of mulch, Dudley and her team were able to remove the odor. Through a process known as biochemical oxidation, the microorganisms in the mulch converted a potential contaminant

Petroleum Engineering

As long as there is a demand for oil and gas, there will be a demand for chemical engineers specializing in petroleum engineering. According to *Graduating Engineer Magazine*, the job market for petroleum engineers is excellent, with starting salaries highest among all engineering fields. Graduates can expect to start at $50,000 per year, which indicates how important it is for oil and gas companies to find qualified petroleum engineers. As the field grows, big oil companies like Exxon, Mobil, Shell, and Chevron will seek petroleum engineers for their big projects.

According to Raymond B. Landis in his book *Studying Engineering: A Road Map to a Rewarding Career*, engineers in this discipline "work in all capacities related to petroleum (gas and oil) and its byproducts. These include designing processes, equipment, and systems for locating new sources of oil and gas; sustaining the flow of extant sources; removing, transporting, and storing oil and gas; and refining them into useful products."

A petroleum engineer obtains a sample of gas from an industrial pipeline.

into carbon dioxide and water. Dudley explains, "We generally think of technology as very sophisticated, but microorganisms are advanced and sophisticated, too. By applying the natural capabilities of such microorganisms we were able to solve a problem that was important to neighbors in the community."[53]

Harsh Environments

Combating pollution and creating chemical processes that improve the manufacture of chemicals means that chemical engineers may find themselves working in harsh conditions. Stephanie Sullivan elaborates on the potential hazards of working with chemicals:

> Often you are working around lots of different chemicals, so there is a lot of information you have to know to ensure your safety, as well as the safety of others. I have worked in a variety of environments including oil refineries and chemical plants where you can get exposed to harsh chemicals such as sulfuric acid or ammonia. Breathing in such chemicals or getting them on your skin could be potentially harmful.[54]

Chemicals are not the only concern. Some chemical engineers work underground in mines, others occasionally climb large towers high above the earth, and many must work near large and loud machinery. Each of these conditions has associated dangers such as being buried alive, falling from great heights, chemical exposure, or serious injury from malfunctioning equipment.

During her days cleaning air and water pollution, Dudley often visited wastewater treatment facilities, which required wearing special protective gear in the event that she might fall into a basin of sewage. Sullivan explains how she had to be extremely careful while working around sulfuric acid when she was helping to manufacture fertilizer:

> A small leak in a pipe containing sulfuric acid could really burn your skin. We had inspectors constantly checking the pipes. Safety measures are always in place and protective equipment is used to ensure the safety of each employee. A big part of ensuring the safety of everyone in a tough environment is training people to understand the processes with which they work. I try to help others to understand the processes so that everyone can be safe as well as contribute toward improving them.[55]

Educating the Chemical Engineer

The high school student seeking to make his or her mark in the world of chemical engineering will first need to get a solid education in chemistry. Fortunately, more than 150 colleges around the country have accredited chemical engineering programs. Chemical engineering students should expect to master the principles of chemistry, physics, and mathematics so they can apply these principles to the design, development, and operational evaluation of systems employing chemical processes, such as chemical reactors or energy conservation processes. Students also have the option to specialize in an area such as pollution control or the production of

Ask About ABET

When it is time to apply to college, students will want to aim for those schools with ABET-accredited programs. ABET stands for the Accreditation Board for Engineering and Technology, a group made up of practicing engineers and engineering educators who determine if a program should receive accreditation. Having a degree from an ABET-accredited engineering program will make the engineering graduate much more appealing to future employers and post-graduate institutions. To earn accreditation, a program must meet high standards for students, faculty, curriculum, and administration. Graduates of the program also must be able to demonstrate certain skills and knowledge, while the program adminstrators must prove that there is a process in place that will ensure that the program will improve over time.

Of the more than two-thousand four-year colleges and universities in the United States only about 15 percent have accredited engineering programs. Students can find a list of ABET-accredited programs at the ABET website at www.abet.org. Accredited programs are also published annually in the *ABET Accreditation Yearbook*. Students should keep in mind that just because one engineering program is accredited at an institution does not mean that the rest of the engineering programs are also accredited.

products such as automotive plastics. Because chemical engineers now often use computer technology to optimize all phases of research, computer skills are a critical part of the chemical engineering student's education.

Formula for Success

Although the future for chemical engineers appears bright, tomorrow's job candidates will face stiff competition. According to the *Occupational Outlook Handbook*, the number of openings for chemical engineers is projected to be much lower than the number of chemical engineering graduates. In 2000, chemical engineers held about thirty-three thousand jobs. More than 73 percent of these jobs were in manufacturing industries such as chemicals, electronics, petroleum refining, paper, and related industries.

Graduates may decide to work in the chemical process industry developing, extracting, isolating, and combining chemicals and their by-products. Just a few areas of specialty in this industry include agricultural chemicals; rubber and rubber products; and soaps, detergents, perfumes, fats, oils, and cosmetics.

A chemical engineer uses a computer to run an experiment. Computer proficiency is essential in the field of chemical engineering.

Chemical engineers can also use their training in the electronics industry developing the materials and processes that allow microchips and intricate circuitry to be put together properly. In fact, according to the American Institute of Chemical Engineers Annual Survey of Initial Placement of Chemical Engineering Graduates, the electronics sector was the second-highest employer of B.S. graduates for the academic year 2000–2001, and the lead employer for graduates with master's degrees.

Other industries that hire chemical engineers include the food and beverage industry; the environmental, safety, and health industry; the fuel industry; and the design and construction industry. Within the government, the U.S. Environmental Protection Agency, the Department of Energy, the U.S. Navy, NASA, and the Department of Agriculture all employ chemical engineers.

Moneymakers

Chemical engineering graduates will find that the starting salary of a chemical engineer is one of the best among the engineering disciplines. For example, a recent survey of career planning and placement offices of colleges and universities across the country conducted by the National Association of Colleges and Employers (NACE) reported that, between September 2000 and January 2001, the average starting salary offer made to chemical engineering students graduating with a bachelor's degree between September 2000 and August 2001 was $51,572; with a master's degree, $57,887; and with a Ph.D. $73,138. The *Occupational Outlook Handbook* reports median annual earnings of $65,960 in 2000.

Chemical engineers command high starting salaries because it is a profession that has a direct and long-lasting impact on the quality of life on this planet. Chemical engineering is a challenging field that demands a highly motivated individual with a keen eye for detail, discipline, and patience.

Future Opportunities

Chemical engineering offers a challenging and worthwhile career with unlimited potential. For example, chemical engineers of the future may work with other engineers to develop more advanced chemical detection devices that can sense the presence of chemical weapons before they can harm innocent people. According to Sandra Dudley, "In order to develop a chemical detection device known as a 'sniffer' that can identify a chemical attack from a terrorist, a chemical engineer would work with an electrical engineer, a mechanical engineer, and a chemist to determine what technology should be used to detect a particular chemical or a host of chemicals."[56]

Creating the food, clothes, and drugs of tomorrow will also be the job of future chemical engineers. These engineers look optimistically toward the future because as they continue to learn more about chemicals, they will begin to envision newer, better ways to produce chemical solutions to today's problems. For example, while fighting disease and disorders through drugs is certainly effective, chemical engineers are seeking ways to head off disease and disorders before they

Chemical engineers analyze DNA computer models. The study of the human genome is a field of research that holds promise for disease prevention.

set in through a field known as genomics, or the study of genomes—the DNA in an organism. Sullivan explains, "Genomics is a focus of research toward a better understanding of what genes do in the human body. If we have a better understanding of our DNA and certain bad genes—say, the breast cancer gene—maybe there is something we can do to turn that gene off and keep the cancer from starting."[57]

According to Dudley, chemical engineers in the future will be working on perplexing problems involving everyday items. For example, chemical engineers of tomorrow might develop a new plastic that will slow or stop gas from escaping from soft drink bottles. This would prolong the shelf life of soda, which in turn would greatly benefit the beverage industry.

Some chemical engineers solve problems that relate to everyday items like determining how much yeast is needed in a pouch of cake mix. Others tackle more complicated tasks such as devising ways to stop the spread of a chemical weapon before it is unleashed. Regardless, all chemical engineers make a difference by transforming chemical concepts into chemical creations.

Chapter 5

Industrial Engineering: Time Is Money

The phrase "time equals money" should have been coined by an industrial engineer. Almost all businesses can make more money if they operate more efficiently. Industrial engineers know how to make changes that decrease the amount of time it takes to make a product, which usually increases the amount of money a company makes. Raymond B. Landis explains the role of an industrial engineer:

> Industrial engineers determine the most effective ways for an organization to use its various resources—people, machines, materials, information, and energy—to make a process or product. . . . They also design and manage the quality control programs that monitor the production process at every step. They also may be involved in facilities and plant design, along with plant management and production engineering.[58]

Although industrial engineers are educated in the basics of engineering, which means understanding mathematical and scientific principles, they also often serve as the link connecting business management goals and operational performance. By simplifying technical details for nontechnical business decision makers and communicating and implementing methods by which operational workers can follow business strategies and achieve business objectives, industrial engineers are critical to any company.

Industrial engineers improve production processes making reliability, quality, and safety the highest priorities for a company. They determine the best materials needed to make a product, as well as the best way to distribute the finished product to people all over the world. These responsibilities make them essential to any business, which is why industrial engineers can be found with important titles in large companies or as entrepreneurial leaders of their own companies.

An industrial engineer inspects a combustion system for a jet. Manufacturers rely on the expertise of industrial engineers to streamline their production processes.

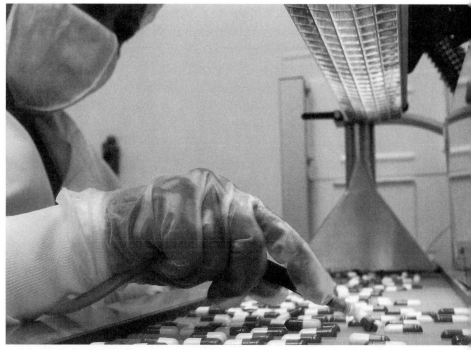

A pharmaceutical worker examines pills at the end of a production line of AIDS medication. One responsibility of industrial engineers is to improve the flow of production lines.

Cheaper, Better, Faster

Industrial engineers create the processes from which new products are made and determine if there are ways to save money while building a better product at a cheaper cost. Virtually every company that manufactures products benefits from the expertise of industrial engineers since they are capable of looking at an existing process and recommending ways to make it better. Michael Sarno, an industrial engineer, explains, "The industrial engineer looks at the picture from head to toe in search of anything that can improve the process. If using a different type of glue to seal two components together or a different type of robot to weld the body frame of a car on an assembly line can generate 2 percent time savings, it could mean a lot of money saved for that company."[59]

The keen eye of an industrial engineer may also lead to the introduction of an entirely new product from an assembly line. According to industrial engineer Michael Gonzalez, an industrial engineer had better be sure that his or her company can make money from producing a new product, because it typically costs hundreds of thousands of dollars to change the component specifications of an automated assembly line. He discusses a well-known industrial engineer with a great idea:

> Lee Iacocca, the famous industrial engineer who designed the Ford Mustang and who later saved Chrysler Corporation from financial ruin, used his industrial engineering skills and vision to design the first minivan. Believe it or not a lot of car companies didn't see the value of building a vehicle roomy enough to carry as much as a van but with a smooth ride like a car. Today, we take minivans for granted, but it took a visionary to break the ice and introduce his concept to mainstream America.[60]

Quality Controllers

Not only do industrial engineers have the foresight to make a new product, they are also responsible for making sure that it is of high quality. Industrial engineers are obsessed with quality, which could involve assessing the effectiveness of huge machinery on an assembly line or paying attention to small, yet significant details in the manufacturing process. For example, in the pharmaceutical industry properly labeling drug bottles, a seemingly minor detail, is critically important. Sarno explains, "No word is more frightening in the pharmaceutical industry than 'recall,' which means that products have to be removed from store shelves because they may be unsafe."[61]

If a certain drug is deemed to have been mislabeled or improperly manufactured, it becomes enormously important to identify and isolate the specific batch of drugs that could be dangerous. Sarno goes on to explain:

> In order to minimize recalls for mislabeling, industrial engineers in the pharmaceutical industry developed a system to photograph the labels of every batch of drugs during the packaging operation. That way, should a problem be detected, the company would be able to quickly identify the batch before it's shipped.[62]

Fortunately, recalls in any industry are few and far between, primarily because industrial engineers implement exacting quality control standards. In fact, industrial engineers spend more time making sure that there is enough quality product on the shelves rather than pulling products off the shelves.

Supply and Demand

Industrial engineers determine how much of a particular product must be supplied in order to satisfy consumer demand. If too much of a product is made, it creates excessive inventory, which costs companies money. If too little of a product is produced, it could create excess demand, which means orders cannot be filled and the company will be perceived as unreliable. According to Sarno, industrial engineers must help companies maintain their image of reliability:

> My company makes products that save or prolong lives, so we have to make sure that our inventory stays at a point so that people who need our products can get our products. That means I have to pay attention to sales forecasts and set up a system that will most efficiently produce the right amount of product to meet demand. I factor in everything including how many shifts of people will be needed on the assembly floor to how many bottles per minute must be filled.[63]

Reliability also requires industrial engineers to calculate the return on investment (ROI) of a company's production efforts, which means measuring how much profit is made after subtracting the costs of raw materials and equipment. For example, before a company spends $5 million on a piece of equipment, it must first determine how many years it will take to pay for that machinery. Some companies, such as the pharmaceutical company that employs Sarno, have time limits, such as three years, to show a profit resulting from an investment in the new equipment. Smaller companies may need to make money sooner and might not be able to afford the investment. Regardless, industrial engineers will be charged with creating "lean" manufacturing processes that enable a company to make enough product to make the purchase of materials worthwhile.

Just-in-Time Manufacturing

In economics nothing could be simpler than the relationship between supply and demand, and nothing could be more difficult, too. Businesspeople struggle with the eternal question of how much of a given product their company should produce. Industrial engineers must come up with a production process that helps a company make exactly the right amount of a product within a specified time frame.

More than thirty years ago, it was easier to be an industrial engineer in the United States, since most companies paid more attention to supply than demand. For example, the American automobile industry made a set amount of cars, then tried to sell them to the public. This left U.S. carmakers vulnerable to competition from Japan where cars were being manufactured much less expensively, mainly because of a philosophy called just-in-time (JIT) manufacturing. Toyota was the first company to develop and perfect JIT, which puts demand before supply. Rather than order more components than necessary to assemble a car, JIT manufacturing dictates ordering parts only after orders for cars come in. It puts a lot of pressure on a company and its parts suppliers to move quickly, but JIT manufacturing leads to the elimination of wasteful inventories and a significant increase in profitability, provided the industrial engineers can make the JIT system work.

Also known as lean manufacturing, JIT manufacturing could backfire. Now that companies can use the Internet to place orders, the speed at which customers expect products to be delivered has increased greatly. If too much inventory leads to a glut forcing companies to lower prices, then too little inventory leads to a shortage, which opens the door for competitors to step in and supply products to meet demand. So getting too "lean" could severely weaken a company to the point of collapse. There may never be a clear-cut answer when it comes to supply and demand, but one thing is certain: Industrial engineers will be at the center of the debate, which is one of the reasons why an industrial engineer's job can be interesting and challenging.

Making the Workplace Safer

It is an industrial engineer's job to make worker safety the highest priority in the manufacturing process. There is a lot of pressure on businesses to make more products faster, which usually means relying on large sophisticated machinery and equipment. Putting humans onto assembly lines always introduces some degree of danger. It is the job of industrial engineers to recognize potential hazards and take steps to minimize the degree of danger and protect people from harm. For example, industrial engineers often call for the installation of emergency stop equipment, which could prevent injury should someone fall into or get part of his or her body caught in a machine.

Michael Sarno recalls how he made a change that greatly improved worker safety. He discovered the danger while supervising workers changing equipment on the assembly line floor to prepare

A steelworker wears protective gear to shield himself from the dangerous conditions of his workplace. Industrial engineers strive to make the workplace safer as well as more efficient.

for the production of a new drug. To prevent equipment used to produce one drug from contaminating the next drug, maintenance workers had to dismantle and clean all the equipment. Sarno explains,

> One worker climbed to the top of a fifteen-foot ladder to remove a 115-pound piece of machinery for cleaning. That was too much weight for a human to hold at such a height with minimal support. He could have fallen or dropped the heavy metal piece on his fellow workers. I led the team that then designed harnesses to be placed around the waist of the worker atop the ladder and around the piece of equipment so that if either fell they would not fall to the ground. I even changed the ladder to a platform, which was much safer and easier to work on. The safety solution cost about $20,000, which compared to the health of a human being, is a small price to pay.[64]

Distribution Decisions

No matter how well or safely a product is produced a company will not make money unless the product can reach its customers, which means devising an efficient distribution system, another critical responsibility of industrial engineers. Many companies that have their own fleet of trucks employ industrial engineers to manage product shipment plans. There are also numerous well-known shipping carriers such as Federal Express and the United Parcel Service that handle shipping responsibilities for companies and people all over the world.

Gerry Birdsall, an industrial engineer with a global shipping company, explains, "A typical dilemma for any shipping carrier is getting time-sensitive packages delivered on time, guaranteed for next-day delivery."[65] According to Birdsall, one of the ways that an industrial engineer can accomplish such a feat is by planning how hubs, or sorting operations, route packages. For example, if a package had to go from Dallas, Texas, to London, England, Birdsall's company would start the process by sorting packages in Dallas according to the shipping carrier's destination point, in this case, the facility in London closest to where the package must be delivered.

Birdsall's team loads packages into destination-specific containers known as "igloos," which are then loaded onto planes bound for airport gateways where the igloos are simply unloaded and transported via trailers to their respective buildings. Birdsall explains: "This process eliminates a lot of additional human handling and that's critical for shipping carriers where even minutes could mean the difference between getting a package or not getting a package where it belongs."[66]

Delivering one package from one point to another might seem simple, but compounding the challenge with millions of packages being sent all over the world requires the excellent organizational skills of industrial engineers. Yet while industrial engineers certainly come up with the process by which packages crisscross the planet, Birdsall believes that successful delivery depends on a combination of the process and the people who actually handle the packages. "An industrial engineer's most important quality is to be able to inspire teamwork. A basketball coach can draw up the greatest plays on paper, but if he or she cannot communicate the strategy to his or her players, or is not seeking the input from his or her players, then the team—or in this case the business—will not succeed."[67]

Human Factors

Not only do industrial engineers strive for input from people about their processes, they study how people function within processes. They often make recommendations to improve the way humans interact with machines, a field of study known as ergonomics. From workers operating assembly line machinery to people driving cars and interfacing with their computers, technology has been made easier to deal with because of industrial engineers. For example, while mechanical engineers may build the engine and structure of an automobile, industrial engineers assess the ergonomics of the automobile, revealing how humans will function while driving, which influences how well a particular brand and style of car sells in the marketplace. According to Michael Gonzalez,

> The main concern of any industrial engineer in the automotive industry is safety, so we are very involved in testing the effectiveness of things like seat belts and air bags. Yet industrial engineers also ensure the comfort and ease of operation of an automobile. We determine if humans can reach buttons on a dashboard and if the seats have enough back support. After all, if people report that a particular car seat

An air bag deploys to cushion the blow to a dummy in a laboratory crash test. Industrial engineers in the automotive industry are responsible for testing the effectiveness of seat belts and air bags.

caused a backache, that brand of car could get a bad reputation. We also make sure that seats are high enough to allow people to see clearly above the steering wheel. We even check to see if the horn is too loud or not loud enough.[68]

In addition to products operated by adults, industrial engineers also improve products used by children, especially toys. Before any toy is mass-produced, industrial engineers make sure that the toy will function in the hands of a child. If a toy cannot be handled properly by a child, it will not sell well and the company producing that toy will lose money. For example, Gonzalez has been hired by toy companies to conduct ergonomic evaluations of their products. He discusses his responsibilities:

I once examined the ergonomics of a video game, which meant assessing the way the buttons on the remote control worked. I had to determine if the game would be able to be played by children. I made recommendations about things like how the buttons should be positioned with respect to the hands of a child. I asked questions like "Will a child understand the function of the buttons? Are the buttons small or large enough in relation to the size of the hands and fingers of a child? Will the video game sit comfortably in the hands of a child?"[69]

As toys for children become more technologically sophisticated, it is likely that industrial engineers will be called upon more often in the future to inspect computer hardware such as keyboards and monitors, as well as software like video games and educational programs.

Bug Hunting

Companies spend a lot of money designing and developing software, but before a software product can be sold to the public, it is the responsibility of experts like industrial engineers to hunt for potential problems or "bugs" (errors in software code) in the system. Every keystroke needs to be checked by industrial engineers to make sure the software does exactly what it was designed to do.

Gonzalez specializes in software quality testing. He has worked with some of the largest companies in the world testing software ranging from video games to programs that help companies collect and analyze sales statistics. Gonzalez explains, "I look at multiple things when conducting a software quality test. For instance, there are big questions like how reliable is the program? How compatible is the software with a computer's operating system? If you insert the CD-ROM to install the software and it crashes your computer, that's obviously not a good thing."[70]

According to Gonzalez, the government and many industries mandate software testing. This means that the field is destined to grow and that industrial engineers familiar with advanced software technologies are likely to be in demand by software companies needing experts to work out the kinks in their products before they are offered to the public.

Raising the Bar Code

Industrial engineers apply new technologies to old systems to save time and money for companies. It was not too long ago that clerks in supermarket checkout lines had to know the prices for every item in the store. If they did not know a price, they would look it up in a catalog or call the store manager over the intercom. Thanks to bar codes—the black lines found on stickers on product packages—that laborious process has been eliminated. Not only were industrial engineers behind such a development, they use that technology in various applications.

For example, Michael Gonzalez once worked for a company that managed furniture warehouses for national companies like K-Mart,

Famous Engineers

Industrial engineers often make great business leaders, but engineers from all disciplines have achieved success and fame in a variety of fields. Of all the well-known engineers throughout history Thomas Edison, Alexander Graham Bell, Neil Armstrong, and artist Leonardo da Vinci top the list. Some of the things people take for granted today are named after the engineers who pioneered them. For example, Dolby sound systems and speakers are the namesake of Ray Dolby, an engineer whose name has become synonymous with high-quality audio. Arthur Nielsen is the man who developed the Nielsen ratings system, which dictates success or failure for television and radio programming.

Other people have gone beyond their chosen technical background to leave their mark on history. For example, several engineers have become world leaders. Herbert Hoover, the thirty-first president of the United States, and Jimmy Carter, the thirty-ninth president of the United States, were engineers. On the other side of the globe, Leonid Brezhnev, once the leader of the former Soviet Union, and Boris Yeltsin, former president of Russia, were both engineers.

One former engineer who demonstrated he could apply technical precision and clear-thinking strategy on the football field was two-time Super Bowl champion coach of the Dallas Cowboys, Tom Landry. Master of film suspense Alfred Hitchcock was an engineer. Hedy Lamarr, the actress best known for cutting Samson's hair in the movie *Samson and Delilah*, was also an engineer, as well as an inventor. Popular TV talk show host Montel Williams and innovative jazz musician Herbie Hancock are also

Macy's, and Bloomingdale's. He was hired to come up with a way to improve the company's warehouse inventory processes. At the time Gonzalez arrived on the job, the warehouse workers wrote invoices and recorded orders on paper. Gonzalez explains,

> It was a paper-intensive environment that required a lot of extra time from employees to handle tedious tasks like making photocopies and filing everything into file cabinets. I conducted a time study to see how long it would take an operator to complete the entire cycle of business from when an order

engineers. And finally one man who stopped being an engineer in order to focus on the comical side of engineering life is Scott Adams, creator of the popular syndicated comic strip "Dilbert."

So while engineering might seem like a specialized field consisting of mathematics and science, it by no means limits someone to a technical job. In fact, judging by the accomplishments of these famous people with engineering backgrounds it is clear that becoming an engineer is a great first step in a career that can take any direction.

Alexander Graham Bell places the world's first long-distance call in 1892. Bell is one of history's most famous engineers.

for a piece of furniture would come in, to when that furniture with an invoice would be shipped out.[71]

From the data Gonzalez collected in his study it became clear that the warehouse needed a new way to improve cycle time, so he recommended a bar scan system similar to the one used in the retail industry. After implementing the bar scan system, the warehouse improved efficiency by 33 percent and productivity by 27 percent. Gonzalez wrote the first training manual outlining the procedures for using the new system and received a promotion.

Good for Business

Industrial engineers often make good business managers. Whether it is shortening an assembly line in a steel factory, figuring out the optimal way to get a package from point A to point B for a shipping carrier, or making sure a hospital has enough beds to accommodate hundreds of patients on any given day, industrial engineers provide logical solutions from which sound business decisions are made. Gonzalez explains, "When you come up with a way to make a better product or a better quality of life within a company or organization, you improve the overall health of that company, which gets you noticed."[72]

Unlike other engineering disciplines in which engineers spend most of their time concentrating on the technical details of their current project, industrial engineers have to interact with upper management, often translating technical information for nontechnical business leaders. In many instances, it is an easy transition for an industrial engineer to advance in a company and assume an executive leadership position.

It is no accident that industrial engineers are capable of moving from engineering to business. Most industrial engineering curriculums in college require students to take basic business courses such as accounting, business administration, finance, and marketing. Perhaps that is why industrial engineers can be found serving as business leaders among some of the world's largest companies, including Amazon.com, the Campbell Soup Company, and Coca-Cola.

Entrepreneurial Engineers

An industrial engineer who does not wish to ascend to a leadership position in a large company may choose to start his or her own business. By being aware of all the elements and processes that comprise the operations of a business, industrial engineers have a solid foundation of technical and business knowledge and are well qualified to become entrepreneurs.

After working with a foreign-based company setting up wide-area and local-area networks (WANs and LANs), Michael Gonzalez decided to create his own company. He explains, "I had a lot of experience in the field and had managed many projects, which often meant setting and meeting budgets."[73] Engineers working in disciplines that tend to be more technical in nature sometimes have no idea how much money they need to complete a project. By not paying attention to budgets, engineers could end up costing employers a lot of money for research and development work that fails to make a profit. Not so with industrial engineers that are trained in the basics of business and who work with businesspeople to make sure projects are completed on time and on budget.

Gonzales is now the president and CEO of Novetix, a company that designs computer database systems. "When I felt ready to start my own business in software systems design and installation I launched Novetix, and I could not be happier. It allows me to make high-level business decisions that determine the direction of the company, but I also like to roll up my sleeves and get involved with the day-to-day work. It's the best of both worlds."[74]

Education

In order to enter the world of industrial engineering, students must first earn their bachelor's degree. There are currently ninety-seven accredited industrial engineering baccalaureate degree programs that take the average student four years to complete. Typically, the first two years are spent studying basic sciences such as mathematics, physics, and chemistry. Also in the first two years, students can expect to take introductory engineering courses as well as studies in the humanities, social sciences, and English. During the last two years, the majority of the student's time will be spent on industrial engineering.

Ideally, an industrial engineering education should equip the student with good math skills, strong time management skills, mechanical skills, creative problem-solving skills, resourcefulness, negotiation skills, leadership skills, and the ability to interact with a diverse group of individuals.

Earnings and Opportunities

Industrial engineering skills are valued by employers in a variety of industries. According to a 2001 salary survey by the National Association of Colleges and Employers, bachelor's degree candidates in industrial engineering received starting salary offers that averaged about $48,320 a year. Master's degree candidates averaged $56,265 a year and Ph.D. candidates, $59,800.

These earnings tend to climb throughout an engineer's career. According to the Institute of Industrial Engineers 2000 Salary Survey, members of the institute reported an average total annual compensation of $76,000, up from 1998's average of $71,000.

Industrial engineers can use their hard-earned skills in a variety of industries as they have a wider window of opportunities than most other engineers. Manufacturing firms and service industries hire a significant number of industrial engineers, but today more and more businesses employ them in fields such as sales and marketing, finance, information systems, and personnel. Industrial engineers

Happy Campers

Engineering camps all over the country offer aspiring young engineers the opportunity to learn about engineering. Students can figure out if engineering is the right career choice for them or they can prepare for their engineering education by spending part of the summer exploring engineering. Many, but not all, of the programs specifically target minority students or female students, or other students traditionally underrepresented in the field.

The summer camp experience gives aspiring engineers the chance to go on field trips to engineering workplaces and research sites and sometimes university departments to meet and learn from engineering professors. Classes, research, experiments, informal workshops, study skills, and presentations by professionals in the field are also often part of the package. Offered by universities and corporations, many of the camps are free and some even reward students with scholarship money or college credit.

An industrial engineer introduces the chairman of Chrysler Corporation (now Daimler-Chrysler) to the Chicago Stock Exchange's computer system in this 1997 photo. Businesses of all types depend on the skills of industrial engineers to improve quality and lower costs.

can also be found at hospitals, airlines, banks, railroads, and in social services. And still others can be found at government agencies or working as independent consultants.

Employers in the manufacturing industry will seek the skills of industrial engineers as long as making a higher quality product as efficiently and as safely as possible is a priority. Because industrial engineers save companies money, they will always be valued by any organization.

Notes

Introduction: Careers in Engineering

1. Raymond B. Landis, *Studying Engineering: A Road Map to a Rewarding Career*, 2nd ed. Los Angeles, CA: Discovery Press, 2000, p.28.

Chapter 1: Electrical Engineering: Robots, Radio Waves, and Solar Panels

2. Harry Roman, interview with author, Newark, NJ, June 2001.

3. Roman, interview with author.

4. Roman, interview with author.

5. Larry Greenstein, interview with author, Middletown, NJ, August 2001.

6. Roman, interview with author.

7. Roman, interview with author.

8. Roman, interview with author.

9. Roman, interview with author.

10. Greenstein, interview with author.

Chapter 2: Mechanical Engineering: Making Mechanical Marvels

11. Landis, *Studying Engineering*, p. 60.

12. Sherita Ceasar, interview with author, Lawrenceville, GA, December 2001.

13. Thomas Maeder and Philip E. Ross, "Machines for Living," *Red Herring*, no. 113, May 2002, p. 43.

14. Mark Hanlon, interview with author, Costa Mesa, CA, April 2002.

15. Hanlon, interview with author.

16. Ceasar, interview with author.

17. Bonnie Dunbar, interview with author, Houston, TX, December 2001.

18. Dunbar, interview with author.

19. Ceasar, interview with author.

20. Ceasar, interview with author.

21. Ceasar, interview with author.

22. Dunbar, interview with author.

23. Dunbar, interview with author.

24. Ceasar, interview with author.

25. Dunbar, interview with author.

Chapter 3: Civil Engineering: Building Bridges, Tunnels, and More

26. Landis, *Studying Engineering*, p. 62.

27. Ed Dauenheimer, interview with author, Cambridge, NY, January 2002.

28. Dauenheimer, interview with author.

29. Walter Konon, interview with author, Newark, NJ, February 2002.

30. Konon, interview with author.

31. Dauenheimer, interview with author.

32. Konon, interview with author.

33. Konon, interview with author.

34. Dauenheimer, interview with author.

35. Dauenheimer, interview with author.

36. Konon, interview with author.

37. Dauenheimer, interview with author.

38. Dauenheimer, interview with author.

39. Konon, interview with author.

40. Konon, interview with author.

41. Konon, interview with author.

42. Konon, interview with author.

43. Dauenheimer, interview with author.

44. Dauenheimer, interview with author.

45. *American Society of Civil Engineers*, "Thinking About Civil Engineering?" www.asce.org.

Chapter 4: Chemical Engineering: The Right Mix

46. Sandra Dudley, interview with author, Atlanta, GA, December 2001.

47. Dudley, interview with author.

48. Stephanie Sullivan, interview with author, Wilson, NC, November 2001.

49. Sullivan, interview with author.

50. Dudley, interview with author.

51. Landis, *Studying Engineering*, p. 68.

52. Dudley, interview with author.

53. Dudley, interview with author.

54. Sullivan, interview with author.

55. Sullivan, interview with author.

56. Dudley, interview with author.

57. Sullivan, interview with author.

Chapter 5: Industrial Engineering: Time Is Money

58. Landis, *Studying Engineering*, p. 69.

59. Michael Sarno, interview with author, Nutley, NJ, March 2002.

60. Michael Gonzalez, interview with author, Newark, NJ, April 2002.

61. Sarno, interview with author.

62. Sarno, interview with author.

63. Sarno, interview with author.

64. Sarno, interview with author.

65. Gerry Birdsall, interview with author, Monmouth Beach, NJ, April 2002.

66. Birdsall, interview with author.

67. Birdsall, interview with author.

68. Gonzalez, interview with author.

69. Gonzalez, interview with author.

70. Gonzalez, interview with author.

71. Gonzalez, interview with author.

72. Gonzalez, interview with author.

73. Gonzalez, interview with author.

74. Gonzalez, interview with author.

Organizations to Contact

American Institute of Chemical Engineers (AIChE)
3 Park Ave.
New York, NY 10016
(212) 591-7338
website: www.aiche.org

AIChE fosters and disseminates chemical engineering knowledge, supports the professional and personal growth of its members, and applies the expertise of its members to address societal needs.

American Society of Civil Engineers (ACSE)
1801 Alexander Bell Drive
Reston, VA 20191-4400
(800) 548-2723
website: www.asce.org

This organization advances professional knowledge, outlines the contributions of civil engineering to society, and improves the practice of civil engineering.

American Society of Mechanical Engineers (ASME)
3 Park Avenue
New York, NY 10016
(800) THE-ASME
website: www.asme.org

ASME promotes and enhances the technical competency and professional well-being of its members through quality programs and activities.

Institute of Electrical and Electronics Engineers (IEEE)
305 E. 47th St.
New York, NY 10017
(212) 705-7800
website: www.ieee.org

The focus of this organization is to advance the theory and practice of electrical engineering and electronics, and computer engineering and computer science.

Institute of Industrial Engineers (IIE)
3577 Parkway Lane, Suite 200
Norcross, GA 30092
(800) 494-0460
website: www.iienet.org

IIE provides leadership in and represents the industrial engineering profession. It also provides resources to those involved in or managing the application, training, education, research, or development of industrial engineering.

Junior Engineering Technical Society (JETS)
1420 King St., Suite 405
Alexandria, VA 22314
(703) 548-5387
website: www.jets.org

This national non-profit education organization serves the precollege engineering community. Through competitions and programs JETS promotes interest in engineering, science, mathematics, and technology, and is dedicated to providing real-world engineering and problem-solving experience to high school students. JETS programs have been recognized, commended, endorsed, and supported by education, engineering, and scientific societies and organizations.

For Further Reading

Books

Nathan Aaseng, *Construction: Building the Impossible*. Minneapolis, MN: Oliver, 2000. Aspiring young civil engineers will be fascinated by these profiles of eight builders and their famous construction projects, including Imhotep and the Step Pyramid, Alexandre Eiffel and the Eiffel Tower, and William Lamb and the Empire State Building.

Celeste Baine, *The Fantastical Engineer: A Thrillseeker's Guide to Careers in Theme Park Engineering*. Calhoun, LA: Bonamy, 2000. A resource book about opportunities in theme park engineering and entertainment engineering, including activities such as scenery fabrication, special effects, fiber-optic lighting design, and pyrotechnics.

————, *Is There a Biomedical Engineer Inside of You? A Student's Guide to Exploring Biomedical Engineering*. Calhoun, LA: Bonamy, 2000. One of a series of books on engineering, this explains what biomedical engineers are, what they earn, which universities have biomedical engineering programs, major areas of employment, and discipline-specific engineering competitions.

————, *Is There a Chemical Engineer Inside of You? A Student's Guide to Exploring Chemical Engineering*. Calhoun, LA: Bonamy, 2000. One of a series of books on engineering, this explains what chemical engineers are, what they earn, which universities have chemical engineering programs, major areas of employment, and discipline-specific engineering competitions.

————, *Is There a Civil Engineer Inside of You? A Student's Guide to Exploring Civil Engineering*. Calhoun, LA: Bonamy, 2000. One of a series of books on engineering, this explains what civil engineers are, what they earn, which universities have civil engineering programs, major areas of employment, and discipline-specific engineering competitions.

————, *Is There a Mechanical Engineer Inside of You? A Student's Guide to Exploring Mechanical Engineering*. Calhoun, LA:

Bonamy, 2000. One of a series of books on engineering, this explains what mechanical engineers are, what they earn, which universities have mechanical engineering programs, major areas of employment, and discipline-specific engineering competitions.

————, *Is There an Electrical Engineer Inside of You? A Student's Guide to Exploring Electrical Engineering.* Calhoun, LA: Bonamy, 2000. One of a series of books on engineering, this explains what electrical engineers are, what they earn, which universities have electrical engineering programs, major areas of employment, and discipline-specific engineering competitions.

————, *Is There an Engineer Inside of You? A Comprehensive Guide to Career Decisions in Engineering.* Calhoun, LA: Bonamy, 2000. A resource for students interested in studying engineering, this guide covers the different branches of engineering, describes where to find engineering-related resources, and provides lists of engineering societies and engineering camps.

David W. Harris, *Truss Fun.* Lakewood, CO: BaHa Enterprises, 2000. This book describes basic engineering principles in a fun and easy manner using simple physics and mathematics. Historic railroad trusses are used as examples.

Matthys Levy and Richard Panchyk, *Engineering the City: How Infrastructure Works—Projects and Principles for Beginners.* Chicago: Chicago Review, 2000. Experiments, projects, and construction diagrams demonstrate how structures such as roads, railroads, bridges, telephone wires, and power lines are constructed.

David Macaulay, *Building Big.* Boston: Houghton Mifflin, 2000. This accompaniment to the author's PBS series of the same title looks at the wonders of the constructed world: dams, domes, skyscrapers, tunnels, and bridges.

Ceel Pasternak, Linda Thornbur, and Sheila Windnall, *Cool Careers for Girls in Engineering.* Manassas Park, VA: Impact, 1999. With ten biographies of women active in the field, this book gives examples of rewarding careers for girls who excel in math and science, such as astrophysicist, aerospace engineer, astronaut, and helicopter pilot. It also gives insights, tricks of the trade, educational requirements, and numerous tips on success.

Websites

American Society for Engineering Education (www.asee.org). This site offers guidance for high school students interested in engineering and engineering technology courses by the American Society for Engineering Education, an organization committed to furthering education in engineering and engineering technology.

Discover Engineering Online (www.discoverengineering.org). This site promotes the engineering profession as a career choice among young people and recognizes the accomplishments of the world's engineers. Provides games, information on what engineers do, their career choices, and frequently asked questions about engineering targeted at K–8 students.

National Engineers Week (www.eweek.org). This site provides information about National Engineers Week, an event that increases public awareness and appreciation of the engineering profession. It has information about the Future City Competition and information for engineers, engineering students, and K–12 students, including relevant links, book lists, and hands-on activities.

Works Consulted

Books

Engineering and Technology Degrees 1999. Washington DC: Engineering Workforce Commission, 1999. The Engineering Workforce Commission is the publications branch of the American Association of Engineering Societies. This report includes comprehensive data on all engineering and engineering tech-nology degrees awarded in the 1998–1999 academic year.

J. Michael Farr, LaVerne L. Ludden, and Paul Mangin, *Best Jobs for the 21st Century.* Indianapolis, IN: JIST Publishing, 2001. This work uses the latest government data to provide information on the best jobs for college graduates in a wide variety of industries and fields.

Raymond B. Landis, *Studying Engineering: A Road Map to a Rewarding Career.* 2nd ed. Los Angeles, CA: Discovery Press, 2000. This book offers a useful introduction to the field of engineering for those students considering a career in engineering and to those students already committed to its pursuit.

Occupational Outlook Handbook. Bulletin 2520. 2000–2001 ed. Washington, DC: U.S. Department of Labor, Bureau of Labor Statistics, January 2000. The *Occupational Outlook Handbook* is a nationally recognized source of career information, designed to provide valuable assistance to individuals making decisions about their future work lives. Revised every two years, the *Handbook* describes what workers do on the job, working conditions, the training and education needed, earnings, and expected job prospects in a wide range of occupations.

Women, Minorities, and Persons with Disabilities in Science and Engineering. Arlington, VA: National Science Foundation, 2000. This report is the tenth in a series of congressionally mandated biennial reports on the status of women and minorities in science and engineering. Both short- and long-term trends in the participation of women, minorities, and persons with disabilities in science and engineering education and employment are documented.

Periodical

Thomas Maeder and Philip E. Ross, "Machines for Living," *Red Herring*, no. 113, May 2002.

Internet Sources

American Institute of Chemical Engineers, Careers and Employment, "2000–2001 Initial Placement of Chemical Engineering Graduates." www.aiche.org.

American Society of Civil Engineers, "Thinking About Civil Engineering?" www.asce.org.

American Society for Engineering Education, "Engineering: Your Future." www.asee.org.

Aprille Ericsson-Jackson, "Career Profiles: Aerospace Engineering," *Graduating Engineer and Computer Career Online*. www.graduatingengineer.com.

National Academy of Engineering, Greatest Achievements of the 20th Century, "Electrification," 2000. www.greatachievements .org.

National Academy of Engineering, "National Academy of Engineering Awards Half-Million-Dollar Prizes for Innovations in Medicine and Education." www.national-academies.org.

National Association of Colleges and Employers, "Salaries to New College Grads Climb in Spite of Slower Economy," 2001. www.jobweb.com.

Shayna Sobel, "The Future of Your Discipline: High Octane Job Market for Petroleum Grads," *Graduating Engineer and Computer Careers Online*. www.graduatingengineer.com.

U.S. Army Corps of Engineers, "Emergency Operations." www.hq. usace.army.mil.

U.S. Bureau of Labor Statistics, "Occupational Employment Statistics: 1998 National Occupational Employment and Wage Estimates—Professional, Paraprofessional, and Technical Occupations." www.bls.gov.

CD ROM

Institute of Electrical and Electronics Engineers, The Sloan Career Cornerstone Series, *Careers for Electrical Engineers and*

Computer Scientists, 1998, 1999. The Sloan Career Cornerstone Series are nine CD-ROMS that provide tools for students, career counselors, professors, and parents who need information to help students make career choices.

Websites

Accreditation Board for Engineering and Technology (ww.abet.org). This site provides information about the Accreditation Board for Engineering and Technology's achievements in quality assurance in engineering, computing, and technology education. The site has relevant information for students interested in learning about the ABET-accreditation process, offers a listing of ABET programs, and provides information for programs and institutions looking to achieve accreditation.

International Federation of Automotive Engineering Societies (ww.fisita.com). The society provides a global forum for engineers representing industry, government, academia, and standardization bodies to ensure that everyone working in automotive transportation is working toward the development of cleaner, safer, more sustainable vehicles.

Index

Picture Credits

About the Authors

Mark Devaney is a public relations professional, college teacher, and freelance writer. Sherri Devaney is a freelance medical editor and former children's textbook editor. They live in Sparta, New Jersey, with their sons Sean and Jeremy.